THE GAME
BEFORE
THE GAME

THE GAME
BEFORE
THE GAME

THE PERFECT 30-MINUTE PRACTICE

Lynn Marriott and Pia Nilsson
with Ron Sirak

GOTHAM BOOKS

GOTHAM BOOKS
Published by Penguin Group (USA) Inc.
375 Hudson Street, New York, New York 10014, U.S.A.
Penguin Group (Canada), 90 Eglinton Avenue East, Suite 700, Toronto, Ontario
M4P 2Y3, Canada (a division of Pearson Penguin Canada Inc.); Penguin Books Ltd,
80 Strand, London WC2R 0RL, England; Penguin Ireland, 25 St Stephen's Green,
Dublin 2, Ireland (a division of Penguin Books Ltd); Penguin Group (Australia), 250
Camberwell Road, Camberwell, Victoria 3124, Australia (a division of Pearson Australia
Group Pty Ltd); Penguin Books India Pvt Ltd, 11 Community Centre, Panchsheel Park,
New Delhi – 110 017, India; Penguin Group (NZ), 67 Apollo Drive, Rosedale, North
Shore 0632, New Zealand (a division of Pearson New Zealand Ltd); Penguin Books
(South Africa) (Pty) Ltd, 24 Sturdee Avenue, Rosebank, Johannesburg 2196, South Africa

Penguin Books Ltd, Registered Offices: 80 Strand, London WC2R 0RL, England

Published by Gotham Books, a member of Penguin Group (USA) Inc.

First printing, October 2007
10   9   8   7   6   5   4   3   2   1

Gotham Books and the skyscraper logo are trademarks of Penguin Group (USA) Inc.

LIBRARY OF CONGRESS CATALOGING–IN–PUBLICATION DATA HAS BEEN
APPLIED FOR.

ISBN 978-1-592-40329-5

VISION54® is a registered trademark of Lynn Marriott and Pia Nilsson.

Printed in the United States of America
Set in Bembo

To the game of golf, thanks for being one of our greatest mentors and providing a special place where we can bring possibilities to life.

—L.M. AND P.N.

For Chris, who makes all things possible.

—R.S.

CONTENTS

FOREWORD

Michael Murphy

Perhaps the greatest disservice that can be done to those who have achieved greatness is to marvel at their accomplishments by focusing on their innate ability alone. While it is certainly true that some are "blessed with talent," not all with such talent achieve greatness, while there are others who do an extraordinary job of mining the ability they have. We all have the potential for remarkable accomplishments, but not all of us exploit that potential. *The Game Before the Game* is a book that helps uncover the path to greatness in golf.

Sure, Tiger Woods and Annika Sorenstam have remarkable physical skills, but those skills go for naught without the focused effort they have each put into developing their abilities. Elite players don't wait for magic to happen, they train for it. They are proactive in learning ways to manage themselves and their performance, especially under pressure. They know that peak performance, while magical or astonishing at times, is a real state that can be trained for. Magic can be made.

The importance of this book is that practice is one of the least understood areas of golf today. Three key questions about practice are usually approached in the reverse order of their importance. Certainly, *what* to practice is essential to determine. More important is to understand *why* you should practice. This is when you begin to merge practice with golf. But the most crucial thing to determine is *how* to practice. Practice needs to equate to the game, not just to the swing. The experience of practice must simulate golf as it is played on the golf course, and it is most successful when it's joyful.

When athletes, or anyone in pursuit of greatness in any area, talk about what it feels like when they are "in the zone," they use eerily similar words that describe something sounding like an out-of-body experience. In fact, what they are describing is a totally integrated experience. Peak performance occurs when all aspects of the individual—physical, mental, and emotional—merge into unified activity. That completely integrated state is a condition that can be pursued. It is a condition that must be pursued.

It is an enormous misconception to think that "being in the zone" is a state into which we stumble. While that is sometimes the case, it is also a state we can create. You can learn how to get into the zone. It is a place you can go to, it is an event you can manufacture. How to practice makes the difference. You practice swing mechanics with mind mechanics. If you don't do them together, the practice might make you worse.

What is the enemy that keeps us from achieving the totally integrated state of peak performance? Simply put, it is distraction. When a coach yells to a player, "Get your head in the game," what is he or she really saying? Be focused. Be engaged. Have your attention directed toward your intention. When you learn to focus your mind it produces wondrous results. *The Game Before the Game* puts you back in touch with why you love the game of golf, and it reveals to you how to best pursue that love.

Here is a mantra to cultivate this: Love something and watch it blossom. What Lynn Marriot and Pia Nilsson have presented here is a road map to get the most from practice, and thereby to get the most from your game. Enjoy the lessons. Make golf a pleasurable and wondrous practice. Surrender to the game. Love golf and watch your game blossom.

—MICHAEL MURPHY

ACKNOWLEDGMENTS

Many golf books talk about how the game provides a place where each one of us can discover what people are really like. Golf books on business say you should always take your prospective client on the course to get a true read on their integrity, character, and behavior. A round of golf can tell you more about a person more quickly than almost any other method of interaction. It may be true that the game reveals where a person is now, but perhaps more significantly the game offers insight and a path to where we are going and what we might become. It's not a crystal ball predicting the future, but more of a place of meditation where our heart and soul reside in knowing we can be more. It is a gift of our potential integral evolution.

We believe the game is an extraordinary place where the possibilities of human potential are offered. The game provides a place where nature and nurture, performance and potential collide. It is a place where each of us can reflect and decide what possibilities we want to pursue and discover our own intimate spirit of the game.

All of this potential is presented with every stroke of a

little white ball in the most beautiful pastures of nature that can be found anywhere on earth. Then again, maybe it's just about putting the ball in a hole. Whatever it is for you, the glorious thing is . . . it's up to YOU to decide.

The Game Before the Game is about developing all the different aspects of our potential with the intention of bringing a fragmented view and experience into an integrated whole. What you practice you get good at and how you practice determines transfer and retention.

We believe if each of us can approach practice as a fun and meaningful journey, it might make arriving at the destination a bit sweeter. Your journey may be about diggin' it out of the dirt, or experiencing the extrasensory joy of knowing you have been there before because you had prepared your nervous system for the vision of success.

Thanks to Ron for yet another special project together. Thank you for being you and for caring so much and taking the time to understand our way of looking at the game. Once again you have been extraordinary in helping us express how the game before the game can be accomplished and enjoyed.

Thanks to our publisher Bill Shinker and editor Brett Valley at Gotham books for believing in our message. You have been a joy to work with.

Thank you to our book agent, Mark Reiter, for making it happen again and guiding us toward the focus of this book. We appreciate your support.

A big heartfelt thank you and deep gratitude to our wonderful friend Elaine Scott. We sincerely appreciate your gentle nudging and guidance in helping us enhance VISION54 to more of its and our potential.

Thank you to the incredible Michael Murphy. You continue to inspire us to take what is implicit and make it explicit and to move the journey forward. As you say: Take the tacit knowing and make it apparent; to love the exploration of why we practice and play.

Thank you to our friends Cindy Davis and Mary Lou Bohn for your support and perspectives. You have both been taking the lead in your different roles as pioneers in the world of golf.

Thanks to all the players we coach and our participants at the VISION54 programs. You are our main source of inspiration to access our potential as coaches.

And thank you to our siblings, Robyn, Mike, Gary, Tomas, and Stefan. You are a special inspiration for us. Thank you for being so supportive and kind to your little sisters. We love you.

LYNN MARRIOTT and PIA NILSSON

Phoenix, Arizona, and Torekov, Sweden

2007

For me, it all starts with Arnold Palmer. If that son of a course superintendent hadn't brought the game to the masses as America moved from the fearful Eisenhower era to the hopeful Kennedy years, this son of a steelworker would have never learned the beauty of the game. Palmer was a local hero where I grew up in Western Pennsylvania, and he was a common man who helped take the game out of the country club and onto municipal courses. With all he achieved, with all he won, never did he lose a feel for his roots, and never did he lose his love of the game. In that is a lesson for all of us. For that we all owe him our thanks.

Because of my writing I recently re-established contact with several childhood friends I knew back in New Castle, Pennsylvania. They are a part of my fondest memories on a golf course, those endless hours we spent as kids playing, practicing, and just having fun. Much too late I thank Rick Plonka, with whom I have played more holes than anyone else, a record that will never be broken, for all those hours we spent together. Tim and Tom Birney are still as steady as any two players I have ever seen. All three could beat me then, and that is something time has not changed. We know now how lucky we were then.

Mark Reiter, my agent, is a man of few words but all of them have been absolutely essential to both *Every Shot Must Have a Purpose* and *The Game Before the Game*. He's a scratch player when it comes to doing his job.

The folks at Gotham Books have once again done an extremely comforting job of holding our hands and walking us through the process of making a book. Many thanks to Brett Valley for his editing and endless thanks to Gotham president Bill Shinker, who has a passion for golf that rivals his passion for publishing.

Golf is a wonderful game to be around. At Golf Digest Publishing I am surrounded by incredibly talented people with an inspiring commitment to journalism. And while most of the golfers I cover stand out as exceedingly accessible people in a world of sports that has grown a tad too selfish, the best of the best are the women of the Ladies Professional Golf Association. The LPGA has been more than my beat since 2002, it has been my home. I thank its players, its staff, and its caddies for sharing their talent, their time, and their stories with me. If you haven't seen an LPGA event—go. These girls rock.

Lynn Marriott and Pia Nilsson are far more than collaborators for me. They are friends, they are teachers, and they are an inspiration to try to be better not just at golf but at everything I do. Their genius is in their appreciation of the individual, and in their refusal to build walls around their imaginations. Every time we talk they have something new to add, some inventive lesson or insight to share, something to complement the learning process. Listen closely; they are talking about more than golf. My thanks to them for trusting me with their ideas.

RON SIRAK
2007
South Wellfleet, Massachusetts

INTRODUCTION

Build Your Game by Tearing Down the Wall Between Practice and Play

Ron Sirak

"Live neither in the past nor in the future, but let each day's work absorb your entire energies, and satisfy your wildest ambition."
—Sir William Osler,
Canadian Physician and educator, 1849–1919

While the exercises in this book are designed to fit comfortably into our busy lives, these are not quick fixes. Lynn and Pia don't believe in quick fixes. They believe in thoughtful change that has a long-term impact rather than impulsive actions with a temporary benefit. They are coaches who believe the first step on the road to better golf is to realize you are embarking on a lifetime journey. The joy is found not in the destination, but rather in the pursuit. **Practice is part of the process, it is part of golf.** Think of all it will build for you:

Purpose—Are you working on something specific?

Responsibility—Are you committed to improving and taking action?

Awareness—Are you conscious of where you are?

Concentration—Are you focused on your purpose?

Trust—Are you believing in your plan?

Intention—Are you clear about your plan?

Center—Are your mind and body in balance?

Energy—Are you enjoying the process?

Part of what makes Lynn and Pia's revolutionary VISION54 approach to golf special is that they make learning fun. And part of the way they do that is by keeping the focus on you—the student—rather than on themselves as teachers. In this book you will find exercises that will make you WANT to practice. They will help you develop a practice routine to make you your own best coach. Contained here are a series of "aha!" moments that will make you think, "I can't wait to get to the course to try this!"

The added benefit is, these exercises are not only enjoyable and beneficial, but they are also scaleable—they can fit into *your* busy life, and they work for *your* skill levels. Each chapter ends with a perfect 30-minute exercise for the topic discussed. But the half-hour plan is just a suggestion. You'll figure out what works best for you. Perhaps it's longer, perhaps it's shorter. Lynn and Pia provide the exercises and you figure out how best to use them.

The purpose of these practice routines is to provide pleasurable learning. Lynn and Pia feel if you enjoy practice, it will become a part of your life, and that will make you a better player. It's when you merge golf and practice that you will see real progress in the development of your game. You'll learn in these pages how to stop wasting time on the range and instead play better by preparing better. You'll remember the reason you play is because you love golf, not because you love swing theory. What you will learn in this book is how to apply VISION54 philosophy to practice.

What is VISION54? It is the notion that we can achieve great things if we believe we can achieve great things. It is about bringing possibility to life. On a golf course, that means believing you can birdie every hole—and shoot a 54! This book brings these breakthrough ideas to practice, just as our book *Every Shot Must Have A Purpose* brought them to playing.

The first notion needed in order to get the most out of your practice—to maximize the return on investment for the time and energy you are putting into the process—is that practice IS golf. Separating the two is a mistake made by the beginner right up to touring professionals. Hitting golf balls is not practice. It is merely hitting golf balls. **For practice to be beneficial, it needs to have a purpose, just like a round of golf. Make practice like golf.**

The best way to make what you learn on the practice area carry over to the golf course is to bring the golf course to the range. Change targets when you practice. Change clubs often. Think. All you do when you mindlessly hit balls is groove a sloppy swing and engrain careless thinking. When most people practice, they fall into a haphazard routine that hypnotizes them into a robotic state that is the antithesis of the graceful game of the golf. Lynn and Pia will help you learn how to get away from "scrape and hit" practice to truly productive learning.

The next step in maximizing your Return on Investment (your ROI) in practice is understanding the three types of practice: Warm-up Practice, Maintenance Practice, and Preparation Practice. The first question to ask when you practice is: "AM I HERE?" The intention of the question is to make certain you have brought your mind, body, and spirit with you. By asking, "Am I here?" you are engaging yourself in the process and acknowledging practice is much more than the physical act of swinging a golf club. The second question is: "WHY AM I HERE?" The answer defines the purpose of the particular practice session.

Let's take a look at the three types of practice:

WARM-UP PRACTICE

This is what you do before you play a round of golf. And whether it is a fun round with friends, a club championship match, or a round on the professional tours, it is important to remember that rarely during warm-up does a player suddenly learn something he didn't already know. It is an act of desperation almost guaranteeing failure to try to learn something new in the precious few minutes before you play. The main objective of warm-up practice is exactly that—to warm up the muscles, engage the mind, and create confidence. It is the overture for the fun to follow.

Like everything else in golf, warm-up routines need to fit the individual. Some players don't even look at their ball flight on the range. They just concentrate on making solid contact, or on getting the feel of a 150-yard shot or a 50-yard pitch. **During warm-up you begin to develop a dialogue with the target that hopefully will turn into a daylong conversation with greatness.** Your round of golf begins even before you walk onto the practice range to warm up. You aren't yet marking numbers on the scorecard, but what you do during these important minutes will go a long way toward determining what numbers you record later.

Some players warm up by playing the first hole or the first few holes on the range: Hit driver then 8-iron. Hit 4-iron. Hit driver, 3-wood, pitching wedge. The purpose of the warm-up practice is to get ready for this particular round of golf. It is usually not wise to try to add something new right before a round, unless the purpose of the round is to practice. In simplicity is found truth: Warm-up practice is to warm up.

MAINTENANCE PRACTICE

This is the kind of practice you do to keep your swing and your game performing efficiently. We all let bad habits sneak into our games. When I am playing poorly I do three things I have to constantly monitor myself for. My takeaway gets too quick. My stance gets too wide. Also, I move too far away from the ball and reach for it. These are my responses to pressure. Part of my maintenance practice is to work on takeaway tempo and to stand tall over the ball.

As with all practice, maintenance practice also needs to include some variation so the brain gets as much of a workout as the body—change clubs and change targets frequently—and it needs to be focused. If someone asked what you are working on, would you have an answer? Would you be able to say "tempo" or "balance" or "distance control" or would you merely admit you are just hitting balls?

Part of what you will learn in this book is how to maintain your level of play in 30-minute sessions that will enable you to get the most out of your practice. Maintaining your level will lower your scores by making your performance more consistent. And consistency is the key to good golf. Learn to do regular checkups and watch your handicap go down. Learn to stay focused and stay engaged and your score will go down even more.

By bringing the tools of VISION54 to the learning area, Lynn and Pia will help you understand how to maintain the five areas of practice: (1) The Swing; (2) The Shots; (3) The Body; (4) The Mind; and (5) The Heart. VISION54 helps us understand that the game is much more than merely swinging a golf club. It is Physical, Technical, Mental, Emotional, Social, and the Spirit of the game. Lynn and Pia will show you how to practice each component.

Can you practice not getting angry? Can you practice maintaining your focus? Of course you can. Maintenance practice is the kind of practice you will do most often, and it is the kind of practice that will help you achieve a game that brings you joy.

PREPARATION PRACTICE

Warm-up practice is about warming up, and maintenance practice is about maintaining your skills. Preparation practice is also exactly what the name says. It is about preparing for the future. That can mean three different things.

First, it is essential in preparation practice to simulate golf because you are preparing to play golf. If you create a mental and emotional connection between the practice area and the playing area, you will maximize your ROI. How do you do this? Bring the golf course to the practice area, and bring the practice area to the golf course. Ever watch a basketball or football team practice? One thing they do is spend time scrimmaging. They practice as if they are playing. That needs to be done in golf as well.

The second form of preparation practice involves adding a shot, getting more flexible or stronger, making a swing change, or honing your mental skills. After winning eleven LPGA tournaments in the 2002 season, Annika Sorenstam looked at her statistics and noticed she was sixty-seventh on tour in converting sand saves. She spent the off-season working on bunker play and was second in sand saves the next year. She identified an area where she could knock off strokes and fixed it.

The third form of preparation practice involves getting ready for a specific event in the future. Perhaps you are going to play links golf in Scotland. You can get ready by practicing shots you will need there, like a knockdown shot or the bump-and-run. Say you are going to play in a member-guest tournament and you know there will be people watching you drive off the first tee. How can you prepare for that moment?

There they are: Warm-up, Maintenance, and Preparation—three types of practice that will make you a better player and lower your score. They have different purposes but the same ultimate goal: to make golf a more enjoyable experience. Lynn and Pia have devised these 30-minute drills because they believe **Too much practice can be as detrimental as too little practice.** The point is to be focused, and you are more focused when you are more refreshed.

There is the romanticized notion created first in the stories about Ben Hogan and perpetuated more recently by Vijay Singh that the longer you practice, the better you will become. Lynn and Pia believe that **The more focused you practice, the better you will become.** To hit balls until your hands bleed may lead to nothing more than sore hands. **The point of practice is to play better, not to hit the most balls.**

Lynn and Pia believe 30 minutes is a sensible practice time frame. Remember, the actual time you spend hitting shots in a round of golf is not much more than that. If you shoot 90 and have a 25-second routine, that's only 37½ minutes of actual golf. You can combine some exercises to practice longer if that works for you, or scale down and find out what you can do for 5 minutes that will give you the most value.

The point is to make practice fit your schedule so you can integrate it into your life. The amount of time you practice also can be determined by what kind of goals you have for your golf. You need to be honest here. How long can you be focused? How often do you need to take breaks to stay focused for practice? Practicing longer than a half hour increases the chances that you'll get tired or distracted and bad thoughts that sap your confidence will creep into your mind. Quantity is not quality.

Lynn and Pia's intention is for the exercises in this book to serve as the underpinnings of a program to put you on a path to a lifetime of improvement and a lifetime of enjoyment. Golf is a game of passion. How often do you come across someone who is, say, waiting for an elevator and is practicing her swing? How come we never see anyone practicing their bowling approach or their fly-fishing cast in such a way?

There is a magical way in which golf climbs into our being and becomes a part of who we are. The exercises in this book will help you learn how to maximize that passion by making your heart and mind and body perform better as one. **These exercises will help you get the most out of the game before the game, and lead to a more enjoyable—and more successful—golf experience.**

THE GAME
BEFORE
THE GAME

CHAPTER I

Every Practice Must Have a Purpose

"We are what we repeatedly do."

—ARISTOTLE

 SWING KEY: Learn how to maximize your Return on Investment.

There is perhaps no sport in which the transition from the static to the active is as pronounced as in golf. From a starting position of absolute stillness we are asked to transform ourselves into a graceful being of poetic movement. And it is exactly that dichotomy that makes golf both so challenging and so compelling. To unite that duality into a singular, purposeful action resulting in a well-struck golf shot requires the harmonious integration of the mind, body, and spirit.

Another way in which that duality is expressed is that,

as golfers, we are here both to stay the same and to evolve to a more advanced level. Look at Tiger Woods and Annika Sorenstam: They have remained true to their personalities, but they have also evolved through thoughtful, deliberate practice. Both have vastly different bodies, for example, from when they first turned pro, and their games have changed in many ways as well.

But, if you watch film of them as youngsters, you'll recognize the swing—Tiger's is hard with a rapid hip turn and Annika's is rhythmic with a quick head release. The essence remains intact, but through growth, through change, it has been allowed to blossom. The unique signature of their swings has stayed the same as they evolved as players.

The secret is to honor your nature and nurture your growth so you can maximize your ability. Golf is a beautifully complex interaction between you, the club, the ball, the target, the course, the weather, your playing partners, and a host of other elements. The game is a cleverly choreographed dance in which we surrender to the total experience and achieve complete control by learning to let go of that which we can't control. **Every shot is an interaction, not a reaction.**

This intriguingly challenging game is a slow-paced activity in which the passions of life swirl around us. The balance is in finding sweet surrender while maintaining full commitment to our actions and total trust in our decisions. Call it evolution with a purpose. **While change is inevitable, growth is optional. Practice is intentional growth.** It is this game before the game that allows golf to reveal its many dimensions, unfolding like a peacock's feathers into a thing of absolute beauty.

In golf, for change to evolve into growth requires long-term, directed practice. The secret to success is to make work enjoyable so you are always motivated by the challenge. When you are engaged with that level of passion you will be able to maximize your ability. That's true in any activity. Passion cannot be manufactured, but it can be released, nurtured, allowed to grow.

Part of why Tiger and Annika have performed at such a high level is they have a love affair with golf. They enjoy the game, and they enjoy getting better at the game. They don't make a distinction between playing and practice. It is all golf, and it is all part of participating in an activity they love. Don't look at practice as a work area but rather as an extension of the play area. That's a huge attitude shift that pays big rewards.

To be productive, practice has to be more than something you do—it has to be something you are engaged in. It is not just mindlessly hitting golf balls. We practice to achieve something specific, and we set goals to give focus to practice. Success is found in the balance of outcome and process. How do you find that balance? Have a purpose, have a plan.

- Are you *really* preparing to play?

- Are you *really* preparing for greatness?

- Are you *really* preparing as a whole, to play the game in all *its* and *your* dimensions?

- Are you training the state of peak performance?

What do we mean by training a "state?" A state is your consciousness at the moment. You can be awake, and you can be asleep, but you can't be both awake and asleep simultaneously. Your state is one or the other. Performance is all about what state you are in at the time you hit a shot. Ideally, you are in the state of peak performance. To maximize your ROI in practice, you must be fully engaged and know how to create the state of peak performance. When you learn that state in practice, you can achieve it in play.

The game of golf includes physical, technical, mental, emotional, and social elements. The glue that holds it all together is the spirit of the game.

Understanding those components is at the heart of grasping the VISION54 approach to learning. Let's take a look at the components and the elements of each that would be "nonnegotiable" in order to play better golf.

Physical

- Learn to manage your tension levels.

- Master breathing techniques.

Technical

- Learn how to hold the club. Your hands are the only physical connection you have with the club.

- Create a sensation that the swing is about releasing energy toward the target.

Mental

- Every shot requires a commitment to a decision. You can't escape that reality. We refer to the area behind the ball where you make decisions as the THINK BOX. When you cross the DECISION LINE to execute the shot, you are in what we call the PLAY BOX.

- Manage your self-talk. Studies indicate we have more than sixty thousand thoughts a day. What does that little voice in your head say, and what tone of voice does it use? Is it supportive or destructive?

Emotional

- Stay neutral or happy in the post-shot routine. Emotional reactions get stored as memory for future reference and can determine future behavior.

- Focus on what you can appreciate every day. Don't forget you are out there to have fun! Positive emotions make you release hormones that help to access your whole brain.

Social

- Learn to get into your own bubble before every shot. Find a focus that works for you.

- You are the expert on you. Communicate with your support team. How can they best help you achieve your goal?

Each of the three different types of practice are most productive if structured according to the VISION54 blueprint. If your maintenance practice does not include all of the above elements, it will wander aimlessly and produce an insufficient ROI.

Similarly, the future part of your performance practice needs to take in all the elements of golf as well.

Do an evaluation of what you are good at physically, technically, mentally, emotionally, and socially.

This is the most productive form of preparation practice in which you can engage. We can't stress this enough: Understand your game—understand yourself—and discover your tendencies in order to more closely maximize your potential. Be your own best coach. Ask yourself this essential question:

What can be better?

Of all the things that could be better in your game, if you focused on just one, which would have the biggest impact and yield your best ROI?

Do this exercise right now:

List three improvements that would have the greatest impact on making you a better player. Be honest about the time and energy you are willing to commit to practice and then decide how you could get better and score lower the fastest. Is it putting? Iron play? Your temper?

After our VISION54 programs, we ask the participants what was good about their games, and what can be better. It is always fascinating—and quite revealing—to hear what they chose as their ROI focus.

One player we coach, Mindy, decided she could maximize her ROI by focusing on the mental side of the game. She left our program feeling she could improve most dramatically by learning to make clear, committed, and congruent decisions in the think box and then have the courage to enact those decisions in the play box. She knew indecision—a lack of confidence—was hurting her game. By focusing on commitment to her decisions, Mindy was able to lower her handicap from 14 to scratch in two years.

Another player, Steve, decided he could benefit most by focusing on the emotional side of the game. He wanted to learn how to stay neutral or happy after every shot. Steve came to understand he was wasting too much energy being unhappy on the golf course. Not only was this not fun, but it also did not produce very good golf. Steve had been a 1-handicap golfer, then his game fell apart and he ballooned to a 9.

Steve became a very angry golfer locked in a downward spiral of emotions. At our VISION54 program he was able to step outside himself and see what he had become. Four months after committing to his focus—learning to control his emotions on the golf course—he was back to being a 2-handicap. And he even enjoyed the game again!

A third player, Frank, also had a clear "aha!" moment involving his optimal focus. Frank's breakthrough was more of a technical nature, although it also involved a healthy degree of emotional honesty. Frank was overweight and inflexible. He also had no desire to change his eating or exercise habits. His ROI was maximized by focusing on developing a new feel in his swing for what it takes to release energy toward the target for a person of his size. Instead of trying to learn a swing he couldn't make, he committed to making a move that best fit his body. His handicap went from 14 to 9 in two months.

Bill, a 6-handicap, came to our school with an extremely solid short game and was excellent off the tee. His problem was with his irons, which he tended to hit thin or pull. After three days, Bill was able to see that his iron play had nothing to do with his swing and everything to do with his attitude. He became aware that after a good drive he would walk to the ball saying to himself, "I hope I don't pull it again" or "Maybe I should hit a club longer since I might hit it thin." In the pre-shot routine his tension level increased in his jaw and upper body, making it physically impossible to turn properly. Then, when he hit a poor shot, he would react with anger and store the negative memory. Bill's ROI was to improve his self-talk and his emotional reaction to shots. Soon, he broke 80 for the first time.

Each of these individuals found different areas of focus specific to their unique physical and emotional state that would help them improve. They identified a purpose and developed a plan. That's how you maximize your practice ROI. If you had to pick one thing that would have the biggest impact on lowering your score, what would it be?

You can do anything, but not everything. Decide on what would make the biggest difference in your game. Then take action.

One thing we have noticed is that what you practice is what you get good at. If you hit twenty-five consective 7-iron shots, you'll get good at hitting 7-irons. And if you are not focused when you practice, you will become a master at being not focused. Practice putting with three balls and you'll get good at that. But we don't get three chances to putt when we play golf. Ask yourself: What do I want to get good at? Be disciplined in what you choose to practice and be disciplined in how you practice. This is the crucial game before the game, and the only way to retain what you learn is through well-thought-out practice.

The game before the game provides a map of what is possible. Know your goals, evaluate your game, be realistic about how much time you have. Make a plan. Take action. We want deep practice (learn it thoroughly), wide practice (all the factors influencing performance), and real practice (being like golf and staying present in it).

To play your best golf it is important to learn time management, energy management, and state management. Seven seconds in the play box multiplied by your score is not many minutes of actual performance. Practice what you are going to do with all the time you have with "me, myself, and I." How you are going to manage the social implications in the best way possible? Be present for your time.

Deliberate practice is the act of setting clear intentions and paying full attention to those intentions. This requires discipline and enjoyment—you have to want to do it—and the reward will be a sense of appreciation of, and belief in, all the possibilities that exist for your game.

The elements we identified above—physical, technical, mental, emotional, social, and spirit of the game—all need to be integrated into your practice. This is golf's version of cross training. This is how you learn to develop the full person in order to reach your full potential.

As we delve deeper into this book, we want to start you on the proper path by encouraging you to change the way you think about practice. Don't view it as something you dread, but make it an activity you desire. This is something you can control. You have within your power the ability to release the pleasures of practice and to experience it as the "second art" of golf. Embracing the game before the game will allow your game to unfold with all of its potential. Now let's get to work!

The Perfect 30-minute Purpose Practice

- Take the five elements of golf: physical, technical, mental, emotional, and social. For each element, list what you do well.

- For each of those five elements, what could be better for you?

- Which three things have top priority in making you better at getting the ball in the hole?

- What actions can you take to make it happen?

CHAPTER II

Warm Up to the Task

"Don't bother to be better than your contemporaries or predecessors. Try to be better than yourself."

—WILLIAM FAULKNER

 SWING KEY: Understand who you are today.

The fascinating thing about Ben Hogan, the guy who pretty much invented practice, is that the stories about him don't need to be true to be accurate. Hogan stories are really parables: The point is, they make a point. There is one about Hogan on the range back when caddies shagged balls for players, and as the story goes, he hit his caddie with a laserlike 1-iron shot. According to legend, old Ben hit the poor guy three more times before he got to his feet. Probably not true, but the point is this: Hogan was extremely accurate with that 1-iron, and he was extremely focused on what he was doing. He was so committed to practice, he was unaware of the poor fellow shagging balls—except as a target.

The lesson learned from Hogan: Commitment and focus are as important during practice as they are during play. The most common practice golfers engage in—especially recreational golfers—is to warm up for a round. And a major mistake many make is going to the range with a desperate sense that a breakthrough must occur before that round, or even the lesser desire that every shot must be struck perfectly in the pre-round routine. Both are unfocused ideas too broad for warm-up practice and are blueprints for disaster. The expectations for the warm-up must be modest and they must be specific. **Go to the range not expecting magic but understanding that the mundane can lead to magic.**

We called a repairman to check on a piece of office equipment that was not working and laughed when the first thing he did was to see if the machine was plugged in. Hearing our chuckles he said: **"Always start with the obvious and work from there."** Pretty wise advice, actually. In our high-tech world we sometimes try to make things more complicated than they really are. Golf is no exception.

We see many players, both amateurs and professionals, work themselves into a state of anxiety during warm-up. They are excellent at preparing themselves NOT to be confident. The problem is, they worry too much about the result rather than the preparation and state. But how often have you hit it poorly on the range and then played beautifully? And how many times has your ball-striking felt better than ever before the round, only to disappear in the black hole between the range and the first tee?

Let's break it down. What should your purpose be on the practice range before a round of golf? The only intentions that make sense are to warm up and to get confident. If that is your intention, how do you maximize your ROI? The better you know yourself and your game, the better you will understand what *you* need to do to get ready. You might need five minutes, twenty minutes, or an hour; you'll figure out what works best for you to get your body ready and make your mind confident. Try different-length practice sessions and you'll learn what you need. Listen to your body. Monitor your mind.

Every round of golf is a new adventure. In a way we know this, often asking ourselves before a round, "Gee, I wonder how I will hit it today? I wonder which me will show up?" But we get to the range and we don't follow up on that question. **Be curious about this particular day.** Don't come to the course with preconceived ideas. Monitor yourself and become aware of the state you are in. Your game may have to adapt. The warm-up is part of that learning process.

Some days you feel on top of the world. On another

your neck might be stiff or your back is cranky, or you are simply low on confidence. But no matter which "you" shows up, you can still devise a playing focus that enables you to make the most of who you are that day. Pay attention when you get to the range. Take notice, accept yourself, and be your own best coach.

Lynn once saw Amy Alcott, the Hall of Fame player, warm up before the last round of an LPGA event in which she was leading. Amy hit several shanks—the most dreaded shot in golf. Most players would shiver in horror and then set about trying to "fix it." Not Amy. She knew there was no fixing anything in the moments before a round, and she dismissed the shanks as an aberration that was not going to follow her onto the golf course. What happened? Amy played well, and won—without hitting a shank.

Our lives are increasingly spent in a static state: sitting in a chair or car, standing at a machine, and working more with our minds than with our bodies. We also live in such a hectic world that we don't take the time to make a smooth transition from one activity to another. It's rush here, do this, rush there, do that. The bombardment of stimuli and demands makes it easy to get pushed into a state of sensory overload. When this happens we shut down as a survival skill and fall out of touch with the joy of life. Good golf comes from joy.

A thoughtful transition from the chaos around us to the calm within is necessary to play good golf. The ability to make that transition is a skill that can be nurtured through self-understanding. Knowing your body, mind, and swing is the key to getting the most out of your game. What exercises will get your body warmed up, your swing warmed up, and create confidence?

We asked Will, a young professional, what he would do in warm-up before a competitive round if he were preparing to play great golf. This is what he said:

"Swing left-handed and hit shots for a few minutes. That gets me coordinated and I don't have any judgments about myself.

"Then hit some different shots with different clubs to different targets to get ready for the real game. Chip or pitch a ball to a hole and then putt, hit a different pitch or chip and then putt again."

Now he was ready to play.

Fans never see Annika Sorenstam jump rope as part of her warm-up. She does that before she gets to the course. Once at the course, her routine is very specific. She will hit very short putts with one hand, and then finish with two hands. She will putt around the clock—placing six or eight balls in a circle around a hole—and chip to different targets. Her purpose is to get loose, find her tempo, and get target-focused. This is a time to collect herself and not be rushed. She will go through her entire routine on the range and, on her way to the first tee, stop to hit a few more putts.

Anders, a junior golfer from Sweden, was warming up before an event on a hot July day in Atlanta. He had done some stretching and then made a few swings with his 8-iron without a ball. He took a ball and rolled it to a natural lie, picked a target, did his full pre-shot routine, and made the swing. He repeated this three times with a little break between each shot. Anders then proclaimed, "I am ready!"

He needed to get warmed up and confident. That achieved, he stopped because he knew it was ninety-five degrees with suffocating humidity. For a Swede it would be very important to manage energy on a day like that. His warm-up was tailored to himself and to the day.

Dare to be different!

What if something happens to disrupt your warm-up routine? What if you got stuck in traffic or held up at work and only had a few minutes to warm up? What would be your fallback plan?

If Pia had only one minute to warm up, she would close her eyes and take some deep, cleansing breaths. Then she would make a few swings in the rough to sense the club going through the grass and feel the joy of making the swings.

If Lynn had only one minute, she would do hookups (a Brain Gym exercise you will learn later) and go inside her mind to count her breaths and feel something positive in her heart.

What would you do if you had only one minute to warm up? Answering this question will help you identify the crucial areas of your game.

Like everything else about golf, your warm-up will be specific to you. Your intentions are to warm up and get confident, but each individual will find a different path to that goal. Here are some exercises to help you get loose, get confident, and achieve the proper balance for a round of golf.

Breathing: Learn who you are that day by focusing on your breathing. First, pay attention to what the inhales and exhales feel like. Do that for a couple of minutes. If you feel you have too much adrenaline, breathe in to the count of three and out to the count of six. If you feel you are too sluggish and want more adrenaline, do the opposite, make your inhales longer than your exhales. You can also do jumping jacks or jump rope to stimulate adrenaline. By focusing on the breathing, your brain is shaking hands with your body.

Brain Gym: Each part of the brain is designed to perform specific tasks. Here are exercises that will better prepare the different parts of your brain to work together with your body. In a sense, you are creating new circuitry that will give better coordination, a more relaxed focus, better balanced emotions, and clearer thinking—a formula for peak performance.

Try these Brain Gym exercises:

• **BALANCE BUTTONS**—Put your left hand behind your left ear, and your right hand on your stomach. Move your head slowly from side to side with your eyes exploring the horizon. Switch hands and repeat. Why do this? The inner ear canals are responsible for balance. By activating reflex points behind the ear and around the navel, you are reminding your body to achieve a state of balance.

• **THE CROSS CRAWL**—Raise your right leg, bending at the knee so the thigh is parallel to the ground and the lower leg is pointed at the ground. Touch the right knee with your left hand. Repeat this with the opposite leg and continue so that you are marching in place very slowly. Why do this? Moving the left leg activates the right hemisphere of the brain, and moving the right leg activates the left hemisphere. Bringing the arms and legs of the opposite sides of the body together requires communication between the two halves of the brain, which is essential for whole-body coordination.

• **HOOKUPS**—While standing, cross the right ankle over the left. Extend your arms straight out, touching the backs of your hands to each other. Cross the right hand over the left, bringing the palms together, and then clasp your fingers together. Draw your hands into the center of the chest with your elbows at your side. Breath slowly, with your tongue touching the roof of your mouth on the inhale and relaxing the tongue on the exhale. Uncross your feet and uncross your arms and touch your fingertips together waist high. Repeat the exercise, leading with the left ankle and hand this time. Why do this? Wayne Cook devised this exercise to harmonize, calm, and integrate the mind and body. This exercise releases stress and enhances balance and coordination.

Stretch: Wake up the nervous system and turn on your coordination. There are many general warm-up stretches, but it's important to identify the limitations in your body and direct your stretching toward those problem areas. Make sure the stretches are specific to your golf movement, and that they are dynamic with a full-body pattern, not just directed at one muscle group at time. Here are a couple of examples.

- Pretend to skip rope: Make circles with your arms to get them loose.

- Deep squat: Stand with your feet at shoulder width and stretch your arms out in front of you and slowly lower yourself into a squatting position. You can hold on to a pole or golf cart if you need to maintain balance. Repeat several times. This will both stretch and activate muscles that are useful for your golf swing.

- Torso back swing: When you get in a golf posture, cross your arms over your shoulders. While the lower body stays still, rotate the upper body back and through. This stretches all the upper muscles that will be used in making a swing. Make swings with only your arms and feel the tension leave them.

Balance: Hit several shots standing on one foot, or with one heel off the ground. Repeat on the other foot or with the other heel off the ground. Hit some shots with your feet close together. Feel how this helps you find your balance, tempo, and rhythm for the day.

Small to Bigger: If you watch most professionals get ready, they start with smaller shots with a more lofted club and build to full swings with less lofted clubs. Give the body and swing time to wake up. Many professionals start with some putts, then chip for a while, hit full shots, and then end with the putter before going to the first tee. You'll find out what works best for you through experimentation.

Tendencies: It is important to know your tendencies. Do you get quick? Do you easily misaim? Monitor yourself for your most frequent tendencies during your warm-up.

Create a State of Confidence: Do things that make

you feel good. We know players who sing or hum a happy tune to activate their joy. Feel a sense of appreciation that you are going to do something you love—play golf! Let your eyes survey the horizon and take in the beauty around you. Keeping your head up sends a positive message to your body. See, hear, and feel the ball going into the hole, by making one-footers and two-footers. Don't practice missing, practice making. Decide on your playing focus for the day. Is your focus going to be tempo? Temper? Staying committed to your decisions? You decide. Go to the side for a few minutes and imagine yourself playing your best golf. Appreciate the game and all you love about it.

Now we are headed to the first tee and that demon doubt appears. Anyone who is honest admits they get butterflies virtually every time they step onto the first tee box. How do you make that feeling go away? First, admit you are nervous. Then, accept that it is OK to be nervous. Finally, develop a plan for dealing with this sensation.

What do you need to do in the one minute before you step up to hit that will get your emotions in balance? How do you react when you get nervous? If you have a tendency to hesitate, you might want to focus on a very strong finish of the swing. If you start to worry about what other people think about you, you might want to hum your favorite song to get that voice out of your head. If you tend to get too tight under pressure, you might want to focus on a lighter grip pressure. The warm-up is about inducing a state of confidence and feeling ready to play.

The Perfect 30-minute Warm-up Exercise

- Jump rope or do jumping jacks for two minutes.

- Do a Cross Crawl (from the Brain Gym).

- Balance on one leg with eyes closed.

- Make swings with eyes closed and no club in your hand.

- Swing with your feet together.

- Make half swings with a 9-iron.

- Hit several shots to specific targets.

- Putt freely without targets.

- Make one-foot putts.

- Sit down and commit to your focus for the day. Close your eyes, then see, hear, and feel yourself taking action on the commitment. Combine this with a couple of deep belly breaths.

CHAPTER III

Maintaining the Well-Oiled Machine

"The ordinary acts we practice every day at home
are of more importance to the soul than their
simplicity might suggest."
—THOMAS MOORE, IRISH POET, 1779–1852

 SWING KEY: Get better by staying the same.

Perhaps the most challenging aspect of golf is achieving a level of consistent performance. Part of the allure of the game is that everyone at some point hits a perfect shot, and one of the fun things about the passion we have for golf is that it is impossible to explain to a nonplayer the joy experienced when a shot is perfectly executed. The gnawing question, however, becomes: "Why can't I do that all the time?" The ability to repeat success is what separates good players from average players, and great players from good players.

We are all more consistent than we think, and we are all capable of being even more predictable than that. One manner in which most players are consistent is that they get in their own way. Perhaps it's aiming poorly, losing correct ball position in the stance, or thinking too much over the ball, but these are all ways we sabotage our performance.

The fluidity with which the swing of Annika Sorenstam repeats is no accident, and it is not the result of inborn talent alone. It was crafted. It was the result of hard work, and it is maintained by carefully structured practice. Sorenstam's swing—one of the most reliably repeating swings in golf history—would not remain such a marvel if not for a practice program cleverly designed around VISION54 principles and studiously followed.

This is called maintenance practice. It is the work you need to put in to make certain your golf engine keeps humming along in proper tune. Everything—whether organic or mechanical—needs to be maintained in order to function properly. In the case of living systems—and your golf game is such a creature—proper care provides the nurturing environment in which performance grows. **The best get better by developing a relentlessly consistent standard of play.** From this foundation of stability they can grow.

We are dynamic creatures. Things constantly change. That's true in our lives, and it's true in our golf. We all have had a round in which we drove the ball great but putted poorly. Or we putted lights out but couldn't hit a green from 150 yards. Different aspects of the game can be our demon on any given day. We yearn for the day when it all comes together.

Golf is a constant pursuit of this perfection. That's why it becomes such a big part of our lives. Just because you did something well last week doesn't mean you are going to do that same thing well this week. We never play the same round twice. But through properly structured maintenance practice, you can bring a greater measure of repeatability to your play.

There is probably no one who has hit as many practice balls as Vijay Singh. There are also few who get as much out of the time they put into practice as Vijay, and that is because he has a plan. Vijay has built a decade-and-a-half record of competitive consistency because he is the master of maintenance practice.

Automobiles that perform the best and last the longest are those that have been serviced diligently. Got to change that oil every three thousand miles. The same is true for the golf swing. Constant use with careless maintenance can lead to an erosion of skills that is not even noticeable until one day the whole engine just breaks down and you find yourself with a swing that can't find a fairway. Everyone needs to make certain all components of their game get the attention they require.

Watching Vijay at a golf tournament is fascinating, especially on the days before competition begins. That's when Vijay is in full maintenance mode. We once saw a factory with a sign out front touting its flawless safety record: PERFECTION IS NO ACCIDENT. That clever play on words also applies to Vijay Singh's golf.

Watch Vijay's routine. He'll pick out a club, decide on a target, move away from the ball, and assess the target he has selected and the club he has chosen, then decide where his feet need to be positioned to make a proper swing to deliver the ball to the target. Then Vijay will lay a club on the ground slightly in front of where his toes would be at address. This helps him line up properly for the shot. Sometimes Vijay will repeat this process for minutes on end without hitting a shot or swinging a club. He is focused only on making certain his setup is correct.

Proper alignment is one of the areas where we can fall into bad habits very easily. Vijay is not only making certain he is lined up properly, but also reinforcing in his brain what it feels like to be lined up properly. We have seen Vijay in a competitive round get over a shot, look at the target—and then back off. The alignment did not feel right. He reassesses the situation and gets back into the proper stance. None of this has to do with swinging a club—so a club need never be swung in the drill—but it does result in a more efficient result of swinging the club.

While Vijay has maintenance drills that are specific to the things he feels he needs to work on, you will develop your own list as you become better at practice and more familiar with the song of your particular swing and game.

When looking at the elements of golf—the technical, physical, mental, emotional, social, and the "life" of the system, the spirit of the game—what do you need to do in regard to each element to maintain your game? We want you to be very specific and choose only the essential areas for your game. It's not about fifty maintenance things but about identifying a handful of important ones that will give you the greatest ROI.

You can also check on your tendencies. We all have a few technical/physical tendencies that show up in the body and swing. And we have a few mental/emotional tendencies that influence the swing as well. These tendencies have been in our game for years, and will be there in the future. Perhaps your miss is to the right. If you know that is one of your tendencies, then it should also be part of your maintenance practice.

What are the things that need to be included in your maintenance practice checkup? Here's a list of fundamentals to check on a regular basis:

Physical/Technical

- Aiming: Is your clubface pointing at the target?

- Alignment: Are your feet, hips, and shoulders parallel to the target line, or how you want them to be?

- Grip pressure: Do you keep the grip pressure constant through the swing and at the pressure level that works best for you?

Mental/Emotional

- Getting in a good performance state: Do you need to check how well you separate the thinking part before the shot from the athletic act of hitting the shot?

- Post-shot routine: Check your ability to remain without judgment on shots you don't like. Feel the good shots in your heart. Create a memory to use in the future.

What are your two or three most common tendencies technically/physically, and the two or three most common mentally/emotionally? Be specific. Keep a list of a handful of critical things in your game.

Pia tends to let her tempo get too quick and she allows too much self-talk. The little voice in her head says things like, "What is wrong with my game? How will I score?"

Lynn, on the other hand, tends to grip the club too tightly and focuses too much on the past, worrying about a missed putt on the previous hole and ruminating over how many under par she should be.

One tour player we work with has a tendency to let her hips get open. She needs to check that in maintenance practice. Watching her at a recent LPGA event at the end of the day, her hips were open again while she was putting. She realized she was also very tired. When you are fatigued, the tendencies are more likely to show up. This player decided it was better to go home and rest, since she was too tired to have a good purpose with her practice.

The way to get the most out of maintenance practice is to develop exercises directed at your tendencies that will prevent your fundamentals from developing fundamental flaws.

When you understand your tendencies, decide what things you can do at home and what things are essential to do on the green grass. Consider the whole game, and not just your full swing. Maintenance practice for putting would help many of us, for example.

Too many players don't work hard enough to hone their habits or solidify their routine. The very concept is so simple it gets lost in the shuffle. This is how you keep your game simple, and how you make it more reliable. Often when players skip maintenance practice, they play well for some time—even if the ball position has changed or the temper after the shots is getting too negative.

Your body and brain compensate for the flaw that has crept into your game and you don't notice anything until it gets quite bad and the body can't compensate any longer. Then when you check with your teacher, you find some major work needs to be done to get back to basics.

As difficult as it may be to believe, Jack Nicklaus was not always on his game. And when Jack was off, he and his coach, Jack Grout, always went back to fundamentals. It is by refamiliarizing ourselves with our routine that we can be better positioned to achieve that which is far from routine.

"Winning is a habit," said the great football coach Vince Lombardi. "Unfortunately, so is losing," he added. Or, as the seventeenth-century poet John Dryden said: "We first make our habits, and then our habits make us."

The Perfect 30-minute Maintenance Exercise

- **Aim maintenance:** Pick a target. Get in your setup position. Now step away while keeping the club behind the ball and aimed the way you aimed it. Is it on target? Do this five times with different clubs to different targets.

- **Tempo maintenance:** Make eight swings alternating between 50 percent of full tempo and 100 percent. Get the feel of shifting tempos with your swing.

- **Commitment Maintenance:** Put a club or a string on the ground behind the ball perpendicular to the target so you need to step over it to address the ball. Hit eight shots to different targets with different clubs and make sure you have made a clear, congruent, committed decision about the shot before stepping over the line, and then stay totally committed to that decision throughout the swing.

- **Distance-feel maintenance:** Put your towel and head covers on the ground at 10, 20, 30, 40, and 50 yards. Hit ten pitch shots to carry to each distance. Do your full routine for each shot.

CHAPTER IV

Prepare to Play Great

"I never think of the future. It comes soon enough."

—ALBERT EINSTEIN

SWING KEY: The future is now.

While warm-up practice gets you ready to play and maintenance practice improves your game by ingraining consistency, the third type of practice—preparation practice—is the most ambitious. Preparation practice has as its focus a goal in the future. It could be getting ready for a certain type of course, it could be adding a specific shot, or it could be a more drastic overhaul of your game.

The results of preparation practice are the least immediate, and because of that, you truly need to stay process-focused and not result-focused. What do we mean by that?

When you are result-focused, you judge success by where the ball ends up or by your score. When you are process-focused, you judge success by how well you stayed committed to something in the process of playing golf or swinging the club. While immediate gratification may be more fun in the short term, delayed gratification produces long-lasting results. Stay focused on the skill you are practicing, and give yourself objective feedback on how you are doing. Many golfers take a couple of practice swings and think the new skill will magically be part of their game. It doesn't work that way.

Pick a focus. Perhaps it's commitment to your decisions, or making a full shoulder turn, or something as basic as your posture.

When you are process-focused, you judge success not by where the ball ended up but by how well you enacted your focus. You can do what you were trying to do and still have the ball end up in a bad place. Usually, it takes many quality repetitions of the process-focus discipline before the ball starts going in the right place.

The most important—and most obvious—thing you can prepare for in preparation practice is playing golf. This seems obvious, but it goes back to what we talked about earlier: Most people go to the range with no sense of purpose. To increase the likelihood that what you learn in the practice area will follow you to the golf course, you need to spend enough time simulating golf in practice.

Our suggestion is that you spend at least half your practice time in some sort of simulated situation. This can involve creative exercises in the practice area, or it can mean taking practice exercises onto the golf course. There are endless fun and imaginative ways you can simulate golf in practice:

- Play six holes in the practice area. Imagine a specific course and hit each shot in the order you would hit it on that course. Do your full routine for each shot, and stay target-focused.

- Set up a nine-hole par-2 course around the putting green. Chip and then putt. Keep score.

- Set up a nine-hole putting course and play it until you finish nine holes under par (fewer than 18 strokes).

- Set up a chipping course and establish as your goal making six consecutive up-and-downs (a chip and one putt). Make each chip shot different.

These are the kind of games children used to play all the time when first learning golf. They saw them not as learning exercises but merely as fun. Unfortunately, many players today get away from golf and get locked in a box of facts. To truly reach your potential you must break the addiction to theory and shatter the obsession with the swing and get back to golf. Tiger Woods says even today in practice he imagines he is playing Arnold Palmer or Jack Nicklaus. Now that's staying in touch with your passion for the game.

Tiger is a throwback to the way golf was learned before it became a classroom activity. His emotional connection to the game is inspiring. The year 2006 was truly a tale of two seasons for Tiger. The first half of the year, he was distracted as his father's lengthy fight with cancer entered its final stages, culminating with his death in May.

After the Masters in April—a disappointing tournament Tiger desperately wanted to win as a final thank-you present to the man who taught him the game—Woods took nine weeks off from competitive golf. When he returned, it was in the U.S. Open at Winged Foot, and for the first time since he turned pro a decade earlier, he missed the cut in a major championship.

After that second consecutive disappointing effort in a major championship, Tiger took another two weeks off, but this time he filled the break with work directed at a specific goal: winning the next major, the British Open. Woods set about adapting his game for the hard-and-fast conditions always found at a British Open, but that were expected to be additionally magnified that year because of the extreme heat wave baking Britain.

Woods worked on his "stinger" knockdown shot with his 2-iron, a shot that hits a high percentage of the fairways when used off the tee and a shot that would roll a long way on the firm fairways of Royal Liverpool at Hoylake, England. He worked on his bump-and-run game, since high shots around the greens were nearly impossible to pull off because of the tight lies on the short, burned-out grass at Hoylake. And he worked on his lag putting, since he knew that a by-product of links golf is a lot of forty-foot birdie putts.

When Woods returned to the tour at the Western Open, he played well and finished tied for second. Now it was off to England. When Woods saw Hoylake, he knew his preparations were even better than he had planned. His stinger was going to be the shot of choice off the tee. After one practice round Tiger realized the driver would stay in the bag most of the week. In fact, he used it only once in seventy-two holes.

Staying fully committed to the game plan he had developed in practice leading up to the British Open, Woods made his prime goal putting the ball in the fairway off the tee, which he did brilliantly. He hit the fairway on forty-eight of the fifty-six non-par-3 holes, first among those in the tournament. On the fourteenth hole—a 456-yard par-4 where everyone felt the need to hit a driver—Woods hit a 2-iron off the tee, leaving more than 210 yards for his second shot, showing extreme confidence in his iron play. That confidence was rewarded with a holed 4-iron for the only eagle of the week on the hole, and a birdie on Sunday that all but wrapped up the British Open championship.

While golf is a constant battle of trying to stay in the now and not let your head get cluttered with future talk, one of the times you can allow your mind to wander into the future is in preparation practice. Unlike warm-up practice and maintenance practice, preparation practice is targeted at some event down the road. **The key, as in all practice and, in fact, in all play, is to be focused on what you want to accomplish.**

Phil Mickelson is legendary for the amount of time he spends on a major championship course in the weeks before the tournament. At the 2006 Masters, Mickelson carried two drivers—one to hit a fade and one to hit a draw, and it paid off in a victory. Ben Hogan was known to work on one single shot he knew would be demanded of him multiple times on a specific course. We have seen professional players decide there were no 7-iron shots for them on a certain course and take that club out of the bag and replace it with another wedge or a utility club.

All of these examples required not only advance planning but also advance practice. Mickelson, Hogan, and Woods spent hours on the range sharpening shots they knew they would need. If there is a recurring theme in this book, it is the essential concept of our philosophy of golf: **Have a specific purpose, make a clear decision, and commit totally to the path you have chosen.**

What sorts of specific things can you prepare for that will happen next week or next month and you can practice today? Say you have a tournament coming up, perhaps a member-guest. Most people might hit extra balls in the days before the tournament in an effort to get ready, but have you ever considered preparing for the specifics of that event? Perhaps there are going to be spectators on the first tee, or at least other people milling around. Can you get ready for that? Absolutely. Pick a spot in the middle of the range with other people around and imagine you are hitting that first tee ball.

Perhaps you know that the pace of play is going to be extremely slow. How can you prepare for that? What if you take two or three minutes between each shot in the practice area? What will you do during that wait time? Can you come up with mental or physical activities that will keep your mind engaged and also your attitude not agitated at the wait? You don't have to be thinking about golf every second you are on the golf course. Sing. Chat. Think about the dinner you are going to have that night. Then, when it is time for you to play, get in the think box and commit and then step into the play box and execute.

Preparation practice can also be aimed at more ambitious long-range goals. While remaining true to his signature swing—an extremely hard pass at the ball—Tiger Woods twice made significant refinements to his motion in the first ten years of a professional career marked with the kind of success that didn't seem to require any tinkering. And don't be surprised if Tiger refines his swing one more time as he makes the transition into a middle-aged golfer who can't swing with the same fury he employs now. The impressive thing about Tiger is that he was already great and he wanted to get even better.

Similarly, Karrie Webb went through a major swing alteration AFTER making it into the LPGA Hall of Fame at the age of twenty-seven. But, motivated by the separation Annika Sorenstam had created between herself and the former Number 1 in women's golf, Webb took the risk and put in the time to change her mechanics. It took Karrie two and a half years, but she finally found a swing she trusted completely under pressure and returned to top form in 2006 with five victories, including a major championship.

The kinds of swing changes Woods and Webb went through are too complicated, too demanding skillwise, and too time-consuming for most recreational players to attempt. But we can help you learn how to add shots to your repertoire without ruining your fun on the golf course. The key is to not let yourself get overwhelmed by the big picture, but rather **keep the focus on the small details that comprise the big picture.**

You need to be absolutely clear about what specifically you want to improve, and then determine the best practice scenario to achieve your goal. Many golfers are too vague. They say something like "I am going to hit it longer" or "I want to be more consistent." When you are too vague, progress crawls along at a snail's pace and your confidence suffers. Know your ROI and don't let it be open-ended.

Annika Sorenstam provides several examples of this kind of future practice. Following the 1999 season, a year in which she struggled with her putter, she spent six weeks doing nothing but putting. She emerged much better on the greens. Annika also came out of that disappointing 1999 season more fully committed to two other aspects of her game—physical fitness and mental discipline. Through dedication and hard work, she made herself much stronger in both areas. Remember, physical and mental training are important parts of your future practice.

Whether it is getting ready to play links golf or trying to change to being a left-to-right hitter of the ball from a right-to-left player, the ultimate end has a specific beginning and necessary steps along the way. The exercises we give you in this chapter are a template for any new skill or future shot you might want to add. Take the exercise below and adapt it to any specific task you want to work on. Remember, define your purpose and then develop a plan.

The Perfect 30-minute Preparation Practice

- Hit ten shots in 30 minutes imagining these situations. Take a few minutes between each shot, just like golf.

- Pretend you are hitting the last shot into a green on 18 in an important tournament.

- Hit a fifty-yard pitch shot.

- Pretend you have a four-footer to win a match.

- Pretend you need to two-putt from fifty feet to lower your handicap.

- Chip from a bare lie to a hole.

- Chip from a deep rough to a hole.

- Hit an extra-high 5-iron, pretending it is over a tree to the green.

- Hit a knock-down 8-iron, pretending the wind is against you and you are going right for the flag with a front-left pin placement.

- What percentage of shots did you hit the way you wanted to?

CHAPTER V

Build Better Balance

"Pooh looked at his two paws. He knew that one
of them was the right, and he knew that when
you had decided which one of them was the
right, then the other was the left, but he never
could remember how to begin."

—WINNIE-THE-POOH

 SWING KEY: Walk the tightrope gracefully from challenge to success.

G reat artists in any activity have an ability to make
their craft appear so effortless they almost do
themselves a disservice by making what they do
look too easy. When this happens, onlookers fall into the
trap of saying, "Oh, it comes naturally" for him or her. But
the only thing that really comes naturally is that we are all

born with the ability to achieve wondrous things. What we do with that natural ability is up to us. Maximizing our potential, unfortunately, does not come naturally. We have to work at it, and out of that labor genius arises.

Golf is a game that nongolfers tend to underestimate as a skillful sport because it appears to someone who has not tried to play to be easy. Fortunately, the strenuous workout programs of modern players have changed the public perception of golfers somewhat. Now golfers look like athletes. Still, the nonplayer can little appreciate the athletic skill and mental discipline required to stand over a 1.68-inch ball 170 yards from the hole and hit it within 4 feet of a 4.25-inch cup. Sometimes the dance is executed with such grace it's easy to overlook the effort behind the choreography.

The well-executed golf shot is like a well-written story or a perfectly performed ballet: It is the result of the purposeful integration of a variety of skills, a balance of a variety of demands. No matter what swing theory is taught, we believe good balance is essential for any golfer, and balance is a multifaceted goal.

We feel balance exercises should always be included in your maintenance practice, and for many players they should be part of warm-up and future practice as well. Better balance will make your swing function better in all circumstances. Uneven lies will become a lot less daunting.

Windy conditions won't throw your swing off as easily. Balance also helps create confidence, which helps you cope with the pressure of competition.

There are three balance centers in the body, and therefore three ways of maintaining balance.

- **The eyes:** We orient ourselves with our vision. This gives us a sense of place in the world.

- **The ears:** The canals around the ears are the clearing-house for physical balance in the body.

- **The nervous system:** Our body has proprioceptors that send signals to our brain. This is what we call "feel" balance. It's the kinesthetic awareness we have. **Balance is more than standing up; it is also not mentally falling down.** The mind and body must be in balance with each other.

We encourage you to practice your feel balance. The goal of the following exercises is to finish the swing in balance. These exercises get more challenging as you progress. Start with half swings and as you get more proficient at each, make bigger swings. You can use any club in your bag, but it's easier to start with the shorter clubs.

- Hit shots with your feet together.

- Hit shots standing on one foot with the other foot resting on the back of the calf. Repeat on the other leg.

- Hit shots with your feet together and eyes closed.

- Hit shots standing on one foot and eyes closed.

- Hit shots standing on the toes of one foot, switch to the other foot.

- Hit shots standing on the toes of one foot with the eyes closed, switch to the other foot.

- Hit shots with your normal stance and posture but after you address the ball, close your eyes and swing.

An important component in balance is center of gravity. This is an aspect of the game most players never consider. Where is your center of gravity? We find that many golfers have a center of gravity that is too high. That makes it very difficult for them to stay in balance. They tend to tip forward, backward, or sideways.

What does it mean to have a high center of gravity? Imagine all your energy being up in your head, as it is when you think a lot. You are experiencing the situation in your brain and not with your entire body. That is a high center of gravity. Now imagine your energy traveling to the lower part of your body, below the belly button. You feel the rough with your feet, and sense the earth below you. That is a low center of gravity.

Hit some shots with the energy in your head, and then hit some shots with the energy lower. What do you notice? Don't be a "neck-up" person playing golf. The ball is on the ground, not in your head. You need to find the balance between the physical and the mental. One of our students told us: "Balance is that thing I wave at as I go from one extreme to the other!" Don't just wave in passing. Stop and say hello.

Even if you can't go to a practice range, you can improve your balance.

- Stand on one foot in balance for fifteen seconds, rest the other foot on the back of the calf, close your eyes another fifteen seconds. Switch feet.

- Stand in your golf posture on one foot for fifteen seconds, rest the other foot on the back of the calf, close your eyes another fifteen seconds. Switch feet.

- Stand in your golf posture on the toes of one foot for fifteen seconds, rest the other foot on the back of the calf, close your eyes another fifteen seconds. Switch feet.

You can also do all the exercises above making small golf swings without a club. Studies on both touring professionals and amateurs at the Titleist Performance Institute have found a good baseline for this exercise is to be able to keep your balance standing on one leg with the eyes closed for at least twenty-five seconds.

Balance is a word that hits at the heart of what golf is all about. The word applies to all aspects of the game, and all aspects of our self. *Balance* refers to the physical equilibrium needed to execute a proper golf swing, but it also applies to the emotional stability needed for clear, committed decision making. **Balance describes the harmony that must exist between the mind and the body, as well as the communication that must go on between the two hemispheres of the brain, in order to play great golf.** Let's look at some applications of balance to golf.

Whenever you are practicing, there are two ways to get feedback: externally or internally. There must be balance between the two. If you are practicing your aim and put clubs at your feet as your feedback mechanism, this is external feedback. If you are practicing tempo and using a metronome or an iPod, that is external feedback. Or perhaps you are practicing with balance rods or balance boards. These are all great external ways of getting feedback.

But you also need to cultivate internal feedback. How can we do this? Do the aiming drill without putting the club at your feet to line you up. Pick your target and make your stance. NOW put a club down and see how you did. Instead of relying on the external feedback FIRST to line you up, learn to line up properly internally and then check your aim with the external device.

You can also practice tempo internally, without the help of a metronome. Feel the rhythm with which you want to swing. Hum a song that is in tune with how you want to swing. See your swing with your mind's eye exactly as you want it to unfold. Hear the melody of your own true swing, and dance to it.

Many golfers we see only practice using the external devices. Those devices function in the practice area, but what happens when you go onto the golf course? You can't take a practice aid with you; it's against the rules. You need to rely on your internal awareness. And you can practice developing that awareness.

We see it all the time. Players hit balls for an hour with clubs at their feet to help their aim. Then they go to play and they misaim right away, since they don't have the clubs as a crutch. Don't become reliant on these external devices. Whatever you are practicing, always find internal ways of doing it and then, as help to check on yourself, apply external tools. If you can only be good at one, we suggest you choose the internal over the external.

The trend now is toward external devices instead of internal. Why? Perhaps because the internal ways are free, and can't be sold. And perhaps that's why a lot of young players produced by this thinking are technically sound—and have poorly developed feel. They are out of balance.

There is also inner and outer balance. That means you want to be good at sensing things that are both inside your skin and outside your skin. We need both to play great golf. What we wrote above about the external and internal feedback is part of this. But it goes way beyond that. You want your physical training to reflect both as well. For example, doing slow-motion exercises with your eyes closed can put you in touch with your body and the finer muscle fibers. Hitting fifty consecutive drivers on the range won't do that.

The balance between inner and outer is crucial. If you are not inner aware you can't sense tempo, tension, your thoughts, and your feelings. You are half a player. And if you are not outer aware you cannot connect to the target, understand the state of your opponent, factor in the weather, or have an idea what your swing looks like.

Yet another form of balance is front and back balance. Think if it this way: Front balance is the display window the world can see. What do you show to the world—to your opponent? Does your body language exude confidence? Do you walk and talk like a winner? You can spot a confident person from one hundred yards away. You can also spot an overly confident person, one who is more likely to try unwise shots.

Back balance is what's inside the store. Sometimes you

walk by a display window and it is unimpressive, but you go inside anyway. Much to your surprise, it's a wonderful store with all the things you like. Who would ever have guessed based on the rather ordinary window display? In golf, this might mean you are a player who is very competent, but has very low confidence. You might have learned some new shots, but you will wait another year before you try them in competition. Even then you still don't think you know the shots well enough.

It's all about balance. You don't want to walk around thinking you are great at everything, when really you need to improve some of your skills. But you also don't want to have a ton of competence without an ounce of courage. In the mind of this person, his game will never be good enough, which means he will never show the full measure of the skills he has.

To take care of a front—the body language that speaks about your game—that is off balance, you need to be open and honest about feedback concerning you and your game. Look at the whole game. Ask someone you trust what they read from your body language on the golf course. Then take action on what you determine will produce YOUR best ROI. To take care of the back, you need to watch your body posture, be proud and walk proudly. You might set up a goal to try something new every week.

How would you rate your balance on a scale of 1 to 5? Do you have a balance between the science and the art of the game? Between internal feedback and external feedback? How about between your long game and your short game? Great players have great balance, just as a great musician has not only tremendous physical skills but also an instinctual feel for the music. The better your balance—in all aspects—the better your play. It's as simple as that.

The Perfect 30-minute Balance Exercise

- Hit shots with feet together for five minutes. (Feel balance)

- Hit shots with your eyes closed after addressing the ball for five minutes. (Feel balance)

- Chip for five minutes standing on one leg; alternate legs. (Feel balance)

- Putt for five minutes toward a hole with your eyes closed after you have addressed the putt and estimate where you think the ball ended up. (Inner awareness)

- Putt for five minutes looking at the target instead of the ball. (Outer awareness)

- Say to a friend five things that you are great at in golf. (Front balance)

CHAPTER VI

Cure Tension with Tempo

"Each team has its own appropriate tempo, a style
of the game best suited to its talents; but within
and around that general score, each individual is
free to elaborate as the spirit moves him."
—MICHAEL NOVAK, WRITING ABOUT BASKETBALL

 SWING KEY: Feel the score of your game and swing to
its melody.

The next time you are at a professional tournament,
go to the practice range and watch the players hit
balls. You'll notice not only a variety of swings but
also a rather wide range of tempos. Just as there is not one
right way to swing the golf club, there is also not one
proper tempo. Tempo, like the swing, is tailored to the individual.

Nick Price, one of the best ball strikers of his generation, has a tempo as quick as a finger snap. Ai Miyazato, the Japanese star on the LPGA, has a swing set to an entirely different clock, one that moves with a slow, hypnotic ease that at first glance could be mistaken for a practice swing. Both Price and Miyazato found a tempo that works for them. Most importantly, they found a way to make the tempo repeat. The real key to tempo is not just its rhythm within the swing but also its repeatability from swing to swing.

As with all aspects of the game, the greater awareness you have of what works for you, the greater your chances are that it will work for you. Awareness of tempo and tension are two factors that, no matter what swing you believe in, will help you swing better. **We all have our own internal clock, and to understand its beat, you must listen and feel.** The more you can feel your swing, the better you will understand your personal tempo, and the more you understand what tempo works for you, the more likely you will be to produce that swing time and time again.

There is so much more to a golf swing than what we can see in photos or by stopping a video to look at angles, lines, paths, and planes. All that can be useful information, but it's not the whole picture. How about the life of the swing—the energy, tempo, rhythm, timing, fluidity, and coordination of the entire motion? That tempo, that flow, needs to be trained and nurtured.

Good arm angles won't help you play better, unless you also have a functioning motion to go with it. Swing theory is like the lines and spaces of a musical staff. It is meaningless without the notes that make the melody of the musical piece.

We see many students who are so focused on technique they never consider that making a swing with a tempo that fits their personality will create more energy and release that energy toward the target. Some players leave that energy in the backswing while others stop it at the ball. It's as if they played the piano with only one hand. Teaching only one tempo is as absurd as teaching only one swing.

As your awareness of tempo and tension increases, you will discover something very interesting: You have more than one tempo that works for you. That seems counterintuitive at first blush because much of what we talk about is having a system you believe in and repeat, but a core belief we have is that golf is a dynamic, always-changing game. Price and Miyazato have tempos within their tempos.

We get a lot of quizzical looks when we tell students we feel it is important to practice different tempos. They overlook the fact that while repeatability is crucial, the game is not played in a laboratory but in the real world. Your body and your swing are different every day to some degree, no matter how small. Sometimes we tease our students and ask: Why do you want a repeatable swing when every shot you hit for the rest of your life is different? You change and the environment changes.

The greatest players are in tune with that. There is a structure to their swing, but it is a flexible structure, like a skyscraper built to sway ever so slightly in the wind. As Tiger Woods, on his way to winning the 2006 British Open at Royal Liverpool, said before one round: "I want to see how the course speaks to me today."

Players who swing and practice with only one tempo can get stuck. There will be many days a particular tempo does not match what your body is ready to do. That's when you have to figure out something else. It's easy to play great golf when you are playing great golf. But the really re-markable players can make great golf out of good golf. We always find that Tiger Woods is at his most remarkable when his usual swing and tempo are not there and he has to piece a round together with what he has.

If you have explored swinging with different tempos you can adjust to what feels right for the day. If you have not experimented with different tempos, you will be lost. Say it's a really cold day and your muscles are tight; the best tempo under those conditions could be 80 percent of your normal swing. Can you make that adjustment?

Or perhaps you have a stiff neck or a sore back and need to scale back to 70 percent. Would you be comfort-able making that change? Inversely, say you get to the golf course and your body feels great, your swing is in synch, and your mind is totally engaged. On a day like that, you might be able to go at the ball at 110 percent. Or perhaps at the end of a tournament round the adrenaline is pumping and you know you need to hit one club less than normal. Can you sense that need? Can you adjust to it?

Structure with flexibility is a good thing in golf! The great players can feel what their bodies are prepared to do. They sense when to downshift and when to push it into fifth gear. You often hear competitors say, "I played within myself today." To play well, that always has to be the case. Successful competitors do a great job of understanding what it means to be within themselves on any particular day.

Elite players, because of their highly refined physical and technical skills, are able to exploit tempo changes in a wider variety of ways. They can, for example, alter their tempo to control the trajectory of the ball flight and the spin of the ball. If you swing with slower tempo, the ball will go lower. This could be very useful on windy days. In the 2006 British Open, Tiger was a master at controlling his tempo, and that mastery translated into his third British Open triumph.

Swinging with a slower tempo with your short irons will enable you to get less backspin. If you play on very soft greens, and you have a tendency to spin the ball too much, this will help. A lot of young players have trouble with this shot, mostly because they don't work on it. When Michelle Wie first started playing professional courses, she would swing a wedge from one hundred yards with the same powerful swing she uses on longer shots and the result was the ball would spin back maybe twenty or thirty feet, sometimes rolling off the putting surface. It goes both ways. If you are chipping from thick Bermuda grass close to the green, you want to be sure to have more acceleration to get through the grass.

Many of the male amateur golfers that come to us have great "aha!" moments while exploring tempo. Since they have never experimented with different tempos, they have never explored alternative ways of making a pass at the ball that might work better. The majority of male amateurs realize that if they drop down a notch in tempo, if they downshift a gear—if they swing easier—they will start hitting the ball more solidly and thus longer. We say you can swing as fast as you want, as long as you can prove to us you can have a good sequence of motion and finish the swing in balance.

The reason we wrote this book is because we don't feel people get enough out of their practice time—that high ROI we discussed. One of the reasons most players don't have a high ROI is because they don't practice some of the things that can most dramatically contribute to lowering their score. One of those essentials is tempo. We bet if you went to a practice area and asked thirty people what they were working on, not one would say "tempo."

Here are some ways to improve your tempo:

- Alternate hitting shots with your driver and your 8-iron. This will help you bring an 8-iron tempo to your driver and make that club more consistent, but it will also help you come to feel the difference in the various tempos you have.

- Pick any club in the bag. Hit it at 25 percent of full tempo. Then hit it at 50 percent of full tempo, followed by 75 percent and 100 percent. In all cases make a full swing. Don't change the length of the swing, just the intensity of the tempo. Maintain the same tempo throughout the swing. Can you feel the difference? Can you control the tempo? Isn't it a wonderful feeling to be able to shift gears like that?

- Pick a distance that is a perfect number for a full swing for a certain club. Say, 150 yards for you is a perfect 7-iron. Can you make full swings with the 6-iron, 5-iron all the way up through your bag and still carry the ball 150 yards? Can you alter the distance the ball goes simply by changing your tempo?

- Hit ten shots swinging as fast as you can while maintaining balance. Turn your 6-iron upside down and grip it below the clubhead. Swing as fast as you can ten times and listen to the sound it makes.

The greatest saboteur of tempo is tension. Some of us carry tension in our hands and forearms, some in the shoulders or the jaws, others in the legs. We were looking at some old photos of Ben Hogan hitting full shots and one of the things that jumped out at us was how relaxed his body posture was. Even in his face there was not a trace of tension as he moved into the impact position.

Hogan was not forcing a swing to happen but rather allowing it to happen. Hogan's primary tempo was relatively quick. But it was his tempo and he trusted it. You want to find out what works best for you and your swing. Here are some different ways to become more aware of your tension levels, so you can prevent it from sabotaging your tempo.

Grip Pressure

Hit six shots with different grip pressures. Start using only three fingers on each hand. Make a smaller swing. Next, put all fingers of both hands on the club, but make the grip pressure as light as possible. Make a swing. For each shot, grip the club a little more tightly. By the last swing, grip it as tightly as possible. The one rule is to keep whatever grip pressure you start with until the end of the swing. Remain constant.

Where in the process did you seem to swing the club

the best and hit it the most solid? Nobody else can tell you how loosely or firmly to grip the club, only you can become aware of what works for you. Some of our students realize they have a tendency to grip it too tightly. Lynn, who tends to grip it too tightly, found hitting shots with winter gloves on was helpful. Others become aware they hold it too loosely, and often need to regrip the club during the swing. These exercises will help you learn the proper grip pressure for you.

Potato Chip Drill

Near the jaw we have the TM joint, which contains more nerve endings than any other part of the body. We found that players who tighten their jaws before swinging or while swinging spread the tension to their shoulders and other parts of the body. This might show up as a constricted shoulder turn, or by throwing your tempo out of whack. If you clench your teeth or tighten your jaw, explore doing it less. Be like Mike. Michael Jordan was so relaxed and confident on the basketball court, he could play with his tongue wagging between his teeth—without the fear he would bite it.

Put a tee between your front teeth and hit some shots. Hit any club in the bag and feel the light pressure against the tee. Another way to do it is to get a bag of thin, crisp potato chips. Put one chip between your front teeth and see if you can hit anything from a wedge to a driver without biting the chip in half.

Slow, Slow, Swings

Make swings at an extremely slow tempo. Let it take two full minutes to complete a swing. Stay present and focused; don't let your mind wander. Keep breathing and notice where in your swing you feel the most tension. Then do the swing again and try to become aware of where in your backswing your back feels tight. Do your forearms tighten up near impact? Now that you've isolated the areas of tension, can you think of ways to lessen it? What needs to be different?

Many players get too static at address. From that position it's easy to get tense. After addressing the ball, try some kind of a waggle with the club, hands, arms, or feet. We have students who sense that their arms at address need to feel more like cooked spaghetti than uncooked spaghetti. Remember, the longer you stand over the ball, the more likely you are to allow tension to form. Don't dawdle. Commit and hit.

The Perfect 30-minute Tempo Exercise

- Hit shots at 25, 50, 75, and 100 percent of full tempo with a 7-iron. Do it three times.

- Take five different clubs, pick a carry distance (140 yards, for example) and see if you can hit all five clubs to the same carry distance.

- Hit five chip shots with different grip pressure. Which one seems best for you?

- Hit ten three-foot putts. Alternate between putts that you want to fall in the cup on the final roll and ones that would end up three feet past the hole if you missed the cup. Can you feel the difference?

CHAPTER VII

Cultivate Creativity

"Talent hits a target no one else can hit; genius hits
a target no one else can see."
    —Arthur Schopenhauer, nineteenth-century
                            German philosopher

SWING KEY: Understand the science, but feel the art.

One of the master technicians of the game was
Ben Hogan. He analyzed every aspect of golf,
blew up his swing after years of fighting a nasty
hook and learned to play a fade game, and could take apart
a course and figure out its vulnerabilities with the best of
them. Even after he quit competition, on the desk in his
office was a physics textbook he used in trying to understand how the golf swing worked. But there was much
more to old Ben than just arm angles, swing planes, and

yardages. He had a feel for the game, and he was a creative genius. We believe you can learn feel and creativity.

Technological advances with clubs and balls have made the game much more enjoyable. But an overreliance on technology in practice develops only the science side of the game and not the artistic side. Feel and creativity need to be cultivated through practice so the golfer and the person can be fully integrated.

Part of the genius of Hogan was that he cultivated both his artistic and scientific sides. That is a common thread in all great golfers, in all great athletes. Hogan was not a fan of knowing yardages. He didn't want to be told which club to hit, he wanted to feel which club to hit. A 150-yard shot might be a 7-iron for Hogan one day on a certain course, and it might be a 5-iron for him another day on a different course. It depended on what type of shot he felt was right under the specific circumstance. That's an acquired skill Hogan developed in part because of the era in which he played—there were no yardage plates or range finders. You had to figure it out yourself.

Another example of how you can develop feel and creativity can be found in how Annika Sorenstam prepared for her appearance in a men's event on the PGA Tour at the 2003 Bank of America Colonial. As part of her practice, she played her home course at Lake Nona from the very back tees. This exposed her to an entirely different set of club choices for approach shots, but it also led to her missing more greens (which she almost never does from LPGA tees) and taught her a wider variety of pitch shots around the greens.

As a junior, Annika didn't like to be creative in her golf game. When Pia was coach of the Swedish National Teams, she wanted her players to finish the day by hitting shots that were low and then high, and by curving the ball left and then right. Annika would stubbornly say, "I will get to that, but first I want to hit it straight from level lies!" As Annika matured as a player she discovered the benefit of hitting a wide variety of shots.

Take Tiger Woods as another example. He is thought of as the premier power player of his generation, and while that is true, what really separates him from his competition is his feel and creativity. His touch around the greens is among the best ever, and his ability to imagine shots is almost otherworldly at times. It is as if he sees shots no one else sees and has an unshakeable belief he can pull off those shots.

Tiger often speaks of how he loves to put the ball in "impossible" lies from the trees and see if he can still make par. It's an exercise he and his father, Earl, used to do when Tiger was a child. And remember that commercial Tiger did where he bounced the ball on a wedge between his legs and behind his back for about thirty seconds before hitting the ball out of midair with a full swing? How do you think he learned that? Simply by having fun on the golf course and experimenting with creativity.

Hogan, Sorenstam, and Woods are players who personify one of the aspects of golf at the core of our philosophy. **We believe that golf is both a science and an art.** While it is important to understand some of the laws of physics and biomechanics, and while having the correct specs on your clubs is crucial, we believe there is much more to the game than the science. To be a player, you also want to practice and nurture the art of the game. **To be good, you must know the rules, but to be great, you must know when to break the rules.** And we are not talking about the rules of golf here, but rather the conventional wisdom of golf.

When Albert Einstein was asked how he came up with the theory of relativity, he said he imagined he was riding through the universe on a beam of light at the speed of light and envisioned what he would see. The imagination came first, and then he used the science to explain it. Our experience with players is that the art of the game has been a victim of the way the game is now learned, and by the tendency to rely on swing theory as the answer to all questions. To find some of the most important answers, you need look no further than inside yourself, or test your imagination and try shots on the course.

We see a lot of players who look as if they should be

great. They are well-conditioned athletes who have mastered what they have been told is a perfect swing and they use the most advanced computers to get the perfect equipment for their swing. Still, they are not playing great golf. Like the tin man in *The Wizard of Oz*, they have created a solidly functioning machine—but one lacking a heart.

What the overly technical approach to learning the game ignores is the fact that nothing is static in golf. You never hit exactly the same shot twice. Never. It's like the Native American proverb about how you can never step into the same river twice because the water is always moving and the river is always changing. It's the same for golf. It's always changing.

It may still be the fifth hole on your home course, but it never plays the exact same way. The lie of the ball can be different, the wind can change, your mental state—the degree of confidence you have at that time—can change. The feel part of your golf game is sensory based. It's what you see, what you hear, and what you feel. Learn to get in touch with that aspect of yourself on the golf course. **Nurture your intelligence, not just your intellect.**

How can you build that sensory feel for golf? Well, we talk a lot about maximizing your ROI, or Return on Investment, in practice by making practice like golf and by using the golf course as a practice ground, not just a proving ground. This a perfect example of how you can significantly improve a crucial part of your game without stepping on the range and mindlessly beating balls. Here are some of the things you can do on the golf course to unleash your creativity and develop it to its fullest:

- Play nine holes and for the first five holes estimate the yardage before looking at the distance on the sprinkler head, in the yardage book, or anywhere else. How close are you to the actual yardage? Did knowing the yardage change the decision you had made about which club to play? Which did you trust more—what your heart told you or what your yardage book told you? What does this tell you about yourself? Play the last four holes without looking at any yardages. Use only your senses to judge distances.

- Play the first three holes by always taking one or two clubs more than you would normally hit on each shot. If a 140-yard shot is a 7-iron for you, hit it with a 6-iron or a 5-iron. Don't try to play a knockdown or bump-and-run shot. Make a full swing and try to carry the ball the distance you wanted it to go with the club you would have liked to hit. Can you feel the swing you need to hit the ball the proper distance? Can you feel there is more than one right shot to hit from this distance?

- Play three holes keeping your eyes closed during the swing or stroke. Do you trust your swing enough to believe you are going to make solid contact and the ball is going to go where you want it to go? Can you feel how the execution of a successful golf shot is connected to this feeling of trust? Before you open your eyes, imagine where the ball ended up. How closely did the result mirror your imagined result?

- Play three holes without a pre-shot routine. Just look at the target, select a club, and step up and hit the shot, feeling total connection to the target. Do this on all shots until you get the ball in the hole. Do you find yourself relying on your instincts more? Do you find the heart, mind, and body working together more successfully? Do you feel you are learning to play the game and not just thinking about how to play the game?

- Play three holes with your feet together on all shots. How does this make you swing the club differently? Does it affect how far the ball goes and change your club selection? Do you find you have to rethink your game and can no longer hit shots by rote? Does this exercise make your brain recalibrate on each shot the way it should anytime you play a golf shot? Does it make you more engaged?

- Play nine holes with only two clubs. Which two clubs would you choose? Why did you choose those two clubs? Would it be fun to play with two clubs one day and a different two clubs another day? What shots did you have to hit during your two-club round that you never hit before? Can you see how this drill stretches the imagination and puts you in a position to develop a trust in your ability to create shots?

- Pick one chip shot to a hole. Chip with every club in your bag and see if you can get them all within a club length of the hole.

- Putt a nine-hole match with a friend without any routine or reading the putts. Just putt and totally trust your feel. Isn't this fun? Do you see how this helps train your mind to imagine different kinds of shots?

These exercises are designed to make you experience the golf course and the shots you hit on it in an entirely new way. The purpose of the exercises is to put you in touch with your creative side. The exercises are designed to make you feel the game. And for the exercises to be beneficial you have to be connected to the results they produce.

That's why it is important to be totally aware of how you are feeling by asking yourself questions. Takes notes. Record your results. Think about what happened during the exercises. Use the information you have gathered. That's developing your intelligence, not just padding your intellect with stats.

The Perfect 30-minute Feel and Creativity Exercise

- Chip with five different clubs to the same hole. How many balls do you get within a club length?

- Putt to different holes. Before the stroke, close your eyes and keep them closed until you have guessed where the ball stopped. Be specific both with distance and direction. If you put a glove in the cup, you won't hear the sound of the ball going into the cup.

- Put head covers at 10-, 20- and 30-yard distances. Hit pitch shots, alternating between the distances, with all your wedges. See if you can also hit the shots with different trajectories.

CHAPTER VIII

Develop Unfailing Focus

"We might believe in free will, but we can hardly be called 'free' if we can't direct our own attention."
—ALAN WALLACE, PH.D.

 SWING KEY: Embrace the moment with total concentration.

O ne of the buzzwords of contemporary culture is *multitasking*. People take pride in being able to do more than one thing at the same time. While admirable in a way, it is also a symptom of the increasingly stressed lives we lead. When you are multitasking, you may be doing more than one thing, but are you doing any of them as well as you can?

The inability to pay attention, or to keep focus, is a modern challenge. We notice it among golfers all the time. They are trying to play their best golf while their mind is on a million other things. To play your best with the skill level you have, you need to pay attention for a few seconds at least. You need to be doing this ONE thing right now.

A lot of this mental wanderlust is hardwired into us. Our minds are restless creatures. They roam constantly, jumping from past memories to future expectations, filled with fantasies, constantly plotting and planning, pursuing pleasures and fleeing fears. The competition we have for our attention is enormous as it is bombarded with stimuli from the computer, newspapers, TV, etc. We live in a world where, if you're not multitasking at a frenzied pace, you can feel left behind.

In golf, you see the impact of this lifestyle when you have a hard time staying present in the play box. It's only a few seconds and still the mind can wander off in all kinds of directions. Perhaps you have committed to a specific playing focus, but then a three-putt or a missed shot causes you to change your mind about your focus and abandon your commitment. We also see players distracted by what others say or do. If your playing partner chooses a 6-iron on a par-3 and you were thinking about a 5-iron, you change your mind right away.

This Golf Attention Deficit Disorder happens in practice as well. Some players practice with an iPod on, denying themselves the opportunity to master an essential of great golf—managing your own thoughts. Or you go to the practice area planning to work on your putting and short game. But to warm up, you start by hitting full shots, and before you know it, you get stuck on the range since you are not happy with how you are swinging the driver. You are no longer paying attention to your intention—working on your short game. What did you come to the practice area to do?

We asked Michael Murphy, the author of *Golf in the Kingdom* and an expert on human potential, what he thought was the most important factor keeping people from shooting 54 or reaching their full potential. Without hesitating, Michael replied: "That's an easy answer. Distraction!"

When we asked Michael how our students can combat distraction, this is what he said:

"Focus on teaching them to get in the zone. It's an event, a psychophysical event. Cultivate the swing and mind together. How to practice makes the difference. You practice the swing mechanics with the mind mechanics. If you don't do them together the practice might make you worse."

We also asked what he would focus on if he were coaching golfers to achieve peak performance. His response:

"First, empowerment of a concentrated mind. I have gone through decades of research. There is a huge amount of data, scientific studies, firsthand accounts of the extraordinary performances of sports legends, surgeons, artists, writers, mothers giving birth, and spiritual leaders, and from all of this a clear pattern has emerged, a pattern of the concentrated mind. The point then is to learn to focus your mind. It produces wondrous results. It gives a huge return on investment. It produces enhanced perceptual abilities and imaginative ability and a greater sense of balance that is subtle but includes extraordinary coordination, flexibility and rhythm and an ability to calm the emotions. It's a recollection of all the fuzzy strands of our wandering minds."

How often do you practice being focused? No one can pay attention all the time. First you need to make choices. What do you want to pay attention to? Then the skill is to know how to pay attention. And finally, learning to know when to pay attention and for how long.

- What is useful to pay attention to before playing a round of golf?

- What is good to pay attention to as you get ready to hit a golf shot?

- What is helpful to pay attention to while addressing the ball and swinging?

How each player experiences their attention is unique to them. **You need to make up your mind to commit**

to focus or you will be one of the distracted golfers who never play as well as they could play.

To play great golf requires efficient energy management. To focus with total attention during a whole round would be exhausting, if not impossible. It's perfectly OK to let your mind wander between shots and go "on vacation," but be present when it is time to play a shot.

We like players we coach to have efficient routines. Do what is essential in your pre-shot routine and get rid of the rest. If you've developed a long, complicated, arduous routine, you'll run out of energy and the fuel to effectively pay attention. When fatigue sets in, the mind has a tendency to wander off into a dialogue with itself about something, and it is usually a dialogue full of self-doubt.

You say to yourself things like:

"I'm losing it. Can I hold on to my lead? Uh-oh, three-putt coming. I'm going to hook this out of bounds. I'm going to choke. That bogey means I need to get it back with a birdie."

This kind of self-talk is not an element of high performance. It creates the self-fulfilling prophecy of failure. Can you practice making this negative self-talk go away? Absolutely. You can practice paying attention.

Training yourself to be attentive is essential to reaching your potential. If you have a tendency to practice mindlessly, hitting shots without thinking, then you are training yourself to be ADD on the golf course. "Practice, rest, practice" is a good motto to follow. Learn to take breaks. How long can you pay attention to what's important? How would you practice if every shot had a purpose?

Lynn has a tendency to let her focus get too broad. When she realizes this is happening she says out loud, "I am going inside now." That is her way of reminding herself to narrow her focus and get into a good internal state. Every player allocates his or her limited attention either by focusing it intentionally, like a laser beam of energy, or by diffusing it in random nonconnected movements.

The shape and content of your golf game depends on how attention is used. Entirely different realities will emerge depending on how attention is invested. A player who can shoot 54 is the one who has the ability to focus attention at will, to be oblivious to distractions, to concentrate for as long as it takes to achieve a goal, and not longer.

Here are a few exercises to learn how to PAY ATTENTION.

- Look at a golf ball, a tee, a blade of grass for forty-five to sixty seconds. How well can you keep your attention? Optimally, your routine should never be longer than that. The actual golf swing only takes about two seconds. Learning to practice your attention like this is a great way to train yourself to have better concentration for each golf shot.

- Sit down comfortably for five minutes and focus your attention on your breathing. If your mind starts wandering, bring it back to your breathing. If you want, you can count your breaths: inhale-one, exhale-two, inhale-three, etc., up to ten and then start over. Stay aware of your breathing.

- Next time you practice, decide on one thing you want to pay attention to. Afterward, check if you did it.

- For the next round of golf, decide on one thing you want to keep your attention on that will help you play well. Perhaps it is a slow takeaway, or finishing the swing. Write it down and decide after the round how well you stayed focused. Make yourself an attention scorecard, and after every shot, mark whether or not you have been paying attention to the one thing you have chosen.

- Eat breakfast and keep your attention on just eating breakfast (not the news, not what you are going to do today, or what new putter you want to buy). Enjoy the taste sensations!

Dr. Anders Ericsson of the Department of Psychology at Florida State University has studied the subject of practice and expert performance for years. His research indicates expert performers in sports, music, writing, chess, and other activities engage in what Dr. Ericsson calls "deliberate practice." Dr. Ericsson explains:

"Deliberate practice is to engage in activities, specifically designed to improve performance, with full concentration. The individuals then actively try to go beyond their current abilities. It's done in limited periods of intense concentration. **Mindless repetition is the direct opposite of deliberate practice.**"

Dr. Ericsson's research also suggests:

- It takes at least ten years of intense involvement (ten thousand hours) in deliberate practice to attain international levels of expert performance.

- Deliberate practice on an elite level is limited to four or five hours a day by the concentration levels that must be maintained to remain fully engaged.

- Finding the appropriate balance between strain and rest is one of the major challenges for individuals pursuing their limits of performance.

- Most individuals never achieve high levels of performance because they are unacquainted with refined, intense, deliberate practice and the complex mechanism mediating expert performance.

- The evidence does not support the myth that hard work at the start will enable one to coast into future success. It most likely reflects confusion between merely maintaining a performance at a high level and continued further improvement of performance.

This is what it means to us:

If you can pay attention for only five minutes in practice, then take a break every five minutes. If you can pay attention for only twenty balls, don't hit fifty. To be able to practice longer and maintain the quality of the practice, train yourself to pay attention for longer periods of time.

We tell our students, "You can practice as much as you want as long as you have a clear purpose and can stay present with that purpose." To count how many balls you hit or how many hours you spend on the range or course doesn't make much sense.

Productive practice is about how present you can stay with your intention and is measured in the quality of the experience as opposed to the quantity of time used or golf balls hit. If you want to be in the zone, you have to "practice" the zone, practice with a concentrated mind.

One of the ways to increase your focus is to invite interference. We have all heard the stories about how Earl Woods used to clap in the middle of Tiger's backswing when he was a child, or would jingle coins in his pocket when his son was putting. The purpose was to develop Tiger's concentration. And when we see the result, there is no doubt Earl's way worked.

You can't learn to manage the interference that swirls around our lives and clutters our heads unless you invite it in, recognize it, and then learn to do something with it. Children don't experience the interference the way adults do. They have the ability to ignore all the stuff going on around them. Adults have a harder time with this. We need to learn how to be the eye in the middle of the hurricane.

It is important to practice handling distractions. They are inevitable. Adjusting to distracting situations requires a commitment to concentration that makes you an overall better player. Anyone—even those with the most restless minds—can learn the focus required to hit high-performance golf shots.

When you play golf, allow the course and your experience on it to be a learning ground and not just a proving ground. If you want to prove something, prove you can stay committed to one playing focus for eighteen holes, no matter what the outcome. This is training focus and concentration. Keep your routine short, and your mind focused. Stay in the present and it will allow for a very enjoyable future.

The Perfect 30-minute Focus Practice

- Make three slow-motion swings (two-minute swings) and pay attention to how present you can stay to your body and swing.

- For twenty minutes on the range, can every shot truly have a purpose? Pick a club, pick a target, pick a shot— and commit! Give yourself a score after the shot on a 1-to-5 scale with 5 being total commitment to the shot. Were you focused?

CHAPTER IX

Practice While Playing

"We judge ourselves by what we feel capable of doing, while others judge us by what we have already done."

—HENRY WADSWORTH LONGFELLOW

 SWING KEY: Make the proving ground a learning ground as well.

Have you ever watched a football team practice? Where do they do it? On a football field, of course. How about baseball or basketball players? And you can sure bet a swimmer is going to do his or her workouts in a swimming pool. Golf is virtually unique among sports in that we create practice areas that are not only separate from the playing area but also radically different in their conceptual challenges. Driving ranges and practice facilities can be very useful if you learn how to make practice like golf. But the best place to learn golf is on the golf course.

Part of the disconnect that has crept into the game is our thinking of the practice area as the learning ground and the golf course as the proving ground. We believe that to fully develop as a golfer you have to learn how to use the golf course as a learning ground as well. Many of the processes of playing the game can be fine-tuned and explored only in the environment of the course. The spontaneity of real play provides lessons that cannot be learned on the practice range.

Rudy Duran, Tiger's childhood golf instructor, told us that when he would take Tiger onto the course, Tiger wanted to play from the same tees as Rudy. So what Rudy did was make up "Tiger par." However many strokes it took Tiger to reach the green, they would add two and that was Tiger par. As Tiger grew and could hit the ball farther, they adjusted the par. Tiger became used to playing golf on the golf course from a very early age and learned the shots you only confront in an actual round. He also got very used to shooting par or under.

The shots that cost us the most strokes—and thus are areas where our ROI for practice time can be the greatest—are shots you only confront on the golf course. There is no out-of-bounds on the practice area. Or intimidating water hazards. Or delicate chips over a bunker to a nearside pin. Or fairways that absolutely must be hit. Or putts that absolutely must be made. These challenges all come in the course of a round of golf. One of the ways we can make practice more like golf is by practicing on the golf course.

How many times have you had to hit a decent drive on a par-4 hole, missed the green with your second shot, and walked to the ball thinking "a good chip and a putt here and I have a par" only to flub the chip forty feet short of the hole and then three-putt for a double bogey? Maybe a better example is that you drive the ball into the right trees, pitch back to the fairway about seventy-five yards short of the green and, with par still very much alive, hit your third shot into the bunker, leave the next shot in the bunker, and eventually make a triple bogey?

These are the situations that drive players crazy—and drive some of them away from the game. Chipping, putting, pitching, and bunker play make up the crucial part of the game. This is where golf gets down to its essence— putting the ball in the hole. Those shots from one hundred yards in are the scoring shots, the place you really save strokes. This is when you have to begin thinking that you are going to either make the shot or make an up-and-down.

Still, as frustrating as it is to throw strokes away when you are inside one hundred yards, how often do you practice these shots? Most recreational players go to the range with their drivers and hit a bucket of balls with the big stick. One way to make you practice these shots is to impress upon yourself how many strokes you are leaving on the golf course.

Next time you play a round of golf, keep track of how many times you have a shot from one hundred yards in. Each time you are in that situation, consider it a par-3 hole. Calculate how many such par-3s you played and how many strokes over or under par you played them. You likely will be startled at the number of strokes you squandered. This is turning the golf course into a valuable practice area.

Certainly, it is not always easy to practice on the course, but there are some creative tools you can use that are not disruptive to other players. You will find that the course offers something the practice area can never produce—surprise. Ever see a professional in a difficult situation and hear a TV announcer say, "Here's a shot you never practice"? Exactly. It's a shot only the golf course can produce.

Let's take a look at some ways to use the course as a practice area.

PURPOSE: STRATEGY AND SHOT CREATIVITY

Play with only one club. Which one do you choose? Can you adapt the club, your swing, and your thinking process to all the shots you have to hit with that one club?

Play with three clubs. Which ones do you choose? Is part of your decision-making trying to leave yourself a shot that is perfect for one of the three clubs you have? Perhaps you want to hit a wedge now so the next shot can be a full 8-iron.

PURPOSE: LEARNING DIFFERENT TRAJECTORIES

Alternate hitting your shot very high or very low. Can you change the trajectory of your shots? Have you ever tried to alter your ball flight? We encourage players to find the simpler ways of doing it. The more it feels like your normal swing, the more likely you are to pull off the shot under pressure. To hit a high shot, play the ball more toward your front foot. To hit a low shot, play the ball more toward the back foot. Make sure you still keep your weight balanced when you move the ball position.

PURPOSE: LEARNING TO CURVE THE BALL

Alternate hitting a fade or a slice and a draw or a hook. The easiest way we know to fade the ball is to open the clubface before gripping the club. To get it to draw or a hook, do the opposite. Make sure the clubface is closed before gripping it. Experiment with how open or closed it needs to be for you to get the desired effect. Also experiment with your alignment. Some players find it useful to align toward where you want the ball flight to start, with the clubface aiming toward where you want the ball to end up. Check it out for yourself.

PURPOSE: TO BE COMFORTABLE WITH THE IN-BETWEEN CLUB SHOTS

How many times have you hit a great drive only to find your approach shot is between what would be a perfect 7-iron and a perfect 8-iron for you? Professionals are amazing at these in-between shots, but most of us never practice them. Here's how you can:

When you play, choose one club longer than the yardage tells you to use. How can you still get it the correct distance? Some players like to grip down an inch on the club and use their normal swing. Some like to make a shorter backswing. Some like to swing with a slower tempo. What is best for you? Figure it out through experimentation.

We hear players coming off the golf course using "awkward" yardages as an excuse for why they didn't score better. "It was so tough today because I was between clubs a half dozen times!" Being between clubs is part of golf. Think of the strokes you can save if you get comfortable with these shots.

PURPOSE: TO EXPLORE YOUR STRATEGY ON EACH HOLE

Play a round and aim for the back edge of the green on every hole. Afterward, reflect on what that tells you about how you play. What did you learn? Did it make you more aggressive in your decision making? Did you learn that sometimes the pin is not the best target?

PURPOSE: TO SHARPEN THE SHORT GAME

Play a round and miss all the greens on purpose. It can be long, short, in a bunker, in the rough. Anywhere. Keep score. How close can you still play to your handicap without hitting a green? What percentage of the time did you chip, pitch, or hit a bunker shot close enough to one-putt? These are the kinds of spontaneous shots that are very difficult to reproduce on the practice area.

PURPOSE: TO EXPLORE YOUR COURSE STRATEGY

Alternate strategies in how you attack each hole. Play one hole in the most aggressive manner you can imagine. How would you do that? Where would you aim? What club would you choose? What speed would your putts have? How do you walk and talk? How does your attitude change? How do you feel?

Now play the next hole as strategically as you can imagine. How would you do that? Where would you aim? What club would you choose? What speed would your putts have? How do you walk and talk? Continue to alternate how you attack each hole.

After doing this exercise, evaluate what you have learned. Which style is more natural for you? How can you learn the other way of playing? To play the best golf possible we need to honor who we are and still at times be able to be more aggressive or more strategic. Did you see that there is more than one way to play a hole, just as there is more than one way to hit a golf shot? Getting better is very much about giving yourself more options.

PURPOSE: TO EXPLORE WHAT IS HAPPENING IN YOUR INTERNAL WORLD AND BRING SILENCE TO IT

Play a few holes in silence. That means externally and internally. No talking to others and no talking to yourself. When you notice your internal chatter start, can you get back to being present and be quieter in your head? There are a lot of tools you can use to turn off this chatter.

Take in the beauty of the course.

Listen to the sounds around you.

Feel a nice feeling in your heart.

Notice your breathing and regulate it.

Feel the sensation under your feet as you walk the fairway.

Was it easy or hard to create silence in your head? How could this skill of being quieter in your mind help your game?

PURPOSE: TO EXPLORE YOUR BODY LANGUAGE AND SELF-TALK

Most players perform a lot better in a more positive state, but that is not true for everyone. We knew one professional who played better when he was a little negative. At those times, he discovered, he was less attached to outcome and swung freer. That revelation was a key to better play for him. Some players can better tap into their adrenaline when they are negative. They need to learn to unleash more adrenaline while maintaining a positive attitude. Pursuing both negative and positive attitudes will teach you a lot about yourself.

Alternate playing holes with different attitudes. On one hole be extremely positive, and on the next be just as negative. If you were the most positive and confident player ever, how would you walk? How would you get ready for a shot? How would you talk to yourself and to others? What would your body language be like?

Play the next hole as the ultimate pessimist. If you were the most negative player and had absolutely no confidence, how would you talk to yourself and others? How would you prepare for the shot? What would your body language be like?

Always finish on a hole where you are positive.

What did you learn? What do you want to do more of while playing? What do you want to do less of or even stop doing? Did you see that attitude is one of those aspects of the game that is controllable?

PURPOSE: CONFIDENCE BUILDER

This is a one-person scramble. Play with two balls from the tee. Pick the best shot and hit two shots from there. Pick the best again and play two shots. Keep doing this until you finish the hole. Keep score and see how low you can go. Can you detect anything you do differently when you hit the better shots?

PURPOSE: TO PRACTICE YOUR MENTAL, TECHNICAL, AND EMOTIONAL TOOLS

This is also a one-person scramble. Play with two balls from the tee. This time pick the one you like the least and play two shots from there. Again, pick the worst outcome of the two and continue until you hole out. Keep score. This exercise can get very difficult. How can you coach yourself to stay neutral or happy and to keep on making clear and committed decisions? Can you keep anger and frustration out of your game?

PURPOSE: TO PRACTICE HOLDING UP UNDER PRESSURE

How do you perceive pressure? Do you have golf in proper perspective? We had a young professional who would remind himself, "I could be in Iraq. Nothing that happens on the golf course can be bad." It is important to feel safe mentally and emotionally when you play. This is not a scary place; it's a beautiful golf course. Practice separating who you are from what you do. You are not your golf score. Your human value stays the same no matter the outcome.

To learn how to handle pressure, you must understand how it affects you. What are your tendencies under pressure? Do you get tight? If so, where? Does your routine get slower? What happens to your tempo? Do you get too tentative? Are you worried about what others will think of you? What tools can you practice to make it better? What is your preferred ball flight? Play it whenever possible under pressure. Under pressure, what "go to" shot do you have the most trust in? Practice and find out.

PURPOSE: TO OPEN UP TO MORE STRATEGIC POSSIBILITIES

This is a fun exercise that will test the bond you have with your best friend. Play with a friend and agree that you are going to make all the decisions about each shot for each other. Your friend decides where you should aim, what trajectory, what club to hit, what type of bunker shot to play, where you should aim your putt, and so on. You do the same for your friend. What did you learn from that exercise?

The Perfect 30-minute On-course Practice

• Pick one of the above exercises and play two or three holes.

    OR

• Play six holes on the range, hitting all the shots you would hit on those holes in the order you would hit them. Play six holes on the course during which:

• Two holes alternate trajectory.

• Two holes alternate curving the ball to the right and to the left.

• Two holes play the "in-between" club shots.

CHAPTER X

Mastery Is Practice

"If there is no struggle, there is no progress."
—FREDERICK DOUGLASS

 SWING KEY: Progress requires patience.

O ne of the challenges of greatness is being judged by an unfair standard. The actions of those who most command our respect are not measured against the actions of others but rather against the performance standard they themselves have established. That's in part why the 2006 season was so frustrating for Annika Sorenstam. She won three LPGA events, including the U.S. Women's Open, but because it was the first time since 1999 she had won fewer than five times, people were asking, "What's wrong with Annika?" For anyone else it was a good year, even a great year. For Annika it was a disappointment.

What made the season especially frustrating for Sorenstam was that she did not play poorly by any reasonable standard. What Annika realized eventually was a reality with which all players must struggle at some point: She was on a plateau. That is a difficult fact to accept, but an important concept to embrace.

Even with great quality practice, improvement in any activity is not an ever-rising diagonal line but rather a move forward by fits and starts. There are also times when a step backward occurs before you are able move forward again. These are challenging times in which it is important to maintain the proper mental and emotional balance, as well as figure out what other learning can take place during a stretch in which it appears as if progress is just not happening.

First, accept that this is a totally natural process. Take a look at a staircase. The path from the bottom to the top is not a straight line. It is a line up, followed by a plateau, and then another line up followed by another plateau. The key is to recognize these plateaus as part of the process. **This is not where you are always going to be, it is merely where you are now.** While learning is happening all the time, improvements in performance look a lot like this:

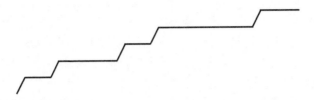

George Leonard has written a wonderful book called *Mastery* in which he describes the essence of mastery and excellence. He points out that all things go through a developmental process that is anything but linear. The first thing, Leonard says, is that we have to embrace the process: Learning is always happening even when you don't see it in your performance.

Athletes and sports teams have hot streaks and slumps. The stock market gets hot and then it cools off. We hear talk of "the real estate bubble," but isn't it absurd to expect that housing prices would continue to rise at the same rate forever?

Similarly, a golfer can't expect to improve EVERY time he or she tees it up. Improvement happens in cycles. Many golfers believe practice will lead to immediate improvement in performance. Nothing could be further from the truth, and no attitude could be more destructive. It's organic and natural to have plateaus. Play the game today as best you can and see what happens tomorrow.

Tiger Woods gets on rolls of incredible performance,

but not even he can maintain that level all the time. And that's what makes those bursts of genius so much fun to watch. And a large part of what makes Tiger and Annika special champions is that they are able to figure out ways to win even when they are on a plateau. It sometimes sounds cocky when Tiger says after a victory, "I had my B-game today," but this often is the case. He embraced the fact he was on a lower rung of the performance ladder and figured out how to get the most out of it.

During a plateau, it is imperative to stay cool and calm and patient. When practicing, be honest and aware of your tendencies and what you need to improve. Sometimes we see a player who is on a plateau, or even backsliding a little, and he says things like "I'm close" or "I'm hitting a lot of great shots but just not getting anything out of it," and he sounds as if he is in denial about the state of his game. Assess your situation realistically.

Don't panic when one of the lulls comes upon you. And be careful whom you listen to. We know players who, when they are struggling, take advice from anyone they play with or meet on the range or in the grillroom. Don't resort to drastic measures and try to make extreme changes in your game. Just because you putted poorly today doesn't mean you have to switch to the claw grip tomorrow.

The next round, or the next shot, might be the beginning of a great leap forward for you. **Stay cool; growth**

can never be forced. Some plateaus are longer than others. Some steps forward are shorter than others. The key is to remember this happens to everyone. The only time a plateau becomes permanent is when you allow it to do so. This can happen to players who don't take the broad view of what impacts performance.

So what do you do when you feel you are spinning your wheels in mud? The approach must be a dual effort that is both mental and physical. First, you have to develop the proper attitude. Tell yourself: "This is a good thing. This is part of the learning process. This is time that can be used for self-evaluation."

We always say that, after a round, you should ask yourself three key questions:

What is good about my game?

What can be better?

How could I do it better?

Do this in all the aspects of golf we have discussed: physical, technical, mental, emotional, social, and spirit in the game. Evaluate yourself and then have a coach/teacher or someone else who observes you play do the evaluation. It's a simple approach, but it can get you on the right track to improvement.

A lot of times you can hit a stale period merely because

you've lost sight of what it is you love about the game. Your passion for the game supplies the energy that keeps the ball rolling. How do you nurture your spirit for the game during these down periods? By asking, "How could golf be more enjoyable, regardless of outcome?" This simple yet complex question can help put you back in touch with your passion for golf.

This evaluation of your game can also help you discover areas of improvement you can practice. Getting better is a big picture made up of a lot of small dots. If you feel you are not getting much out of your game right now, or out of your practice, perhaps it is a time to focus on very specific parts of your game. Bunker play. Chipping. Lag putting. Creating confidence. Committing to decisions. Anything you get better at makes you a better player—and lowers your handicap.

Even more frustrating than hitting a plateau are those times when it seems as if your game has actually gotten worse. In fact, in terms of performance it has. Running into a bit of backsliding is also a natural part of the process of improving. **There is no path to learning that does not involve some slips along the way.** These periods of backsliding are an important time for self-evaluation.

There are many reasons your performance level can drop off. Sometimes your body just needs more time to integrate all you have learned. You know you are doing everything you have learned, but you are not seeing the results. Be patient. Give it time. Sometimes people practice too much. A slumping LPGA player Lynn was coaching showed up with the intention of practicing hard. But after listening to her, Lynn suggested she take two days off and drive to the Grand Canyon to recharge her batteries with the energy of nature's beauty. She came back with an entirely new perspective, practiced, and finished in the top 10 in her next tournament.

Sometimes old habits—or old swing flaws—resurface under pressure, or when you get mentally fatigued. In both cases you lose focus on the changes you have made, allowing the old swing to return. This happens under pressure because the tension of the situation has made you retreat to a comfort zone. In the case of being fatigued it is simply that. The new skill has not failed you, but you have failed the skill by not giving it the concentration it requires, or you haven't had enough time to integrate the new skill into your game.

How should you handle these backslides? Momentum is an incredibly strong force. If you let a downward spiral gain momentum, it can lead to poor play for an extended period of time. Stay patient and be clear on what you want to accomplish. Focus on one or two things that can get you scoring better. Use the tools you have learned from VISION54.

Many golfers panic and abandon their routine when they hit a plateau or backslide. A normal reaction can be to change swing thoughts, putters, or drivers. After a while it gets so confusing it's not a small dip anymore but rather an avalanche cascading into increasingly poor play. Part of what was so impressive about the two major swing changes Tiger Woods went through is that he never lost belief in what he was working on or wavered in his commitment to the process, even when his performance declined.

One young professional we coach, Cecilia, experienced such a backslide her first year on tour and did not handle it as well as Tiger. She tested new clubs constantly, and gathered new swing tips from anyone who came close to her. Needless to say, it wasn't a successful strategy. It can work short term for a couple of days, but it's not sustainable. She had no plan and was merely flailing about, hoping for magic to happen. Remember, growth is planned.

Another typical reaction when you hit a little dip is that you just want to try harder. If you practiced two hours a day, you might change it to four hours. If you hit two hundred balls a day, you go to three hundred. If you work out for twenty minutes, you go to ninety minutes. What happens? Burnout.

Kim, another young professional, had great success early in her career, even winning a major championship. Then a dip occurred. Her reaction was to work harder.

She told us she never dared take even one day off for fear of getting worse. Finally, Kim realized she needed another strategy.

She figured she had to practice well, but that she also needed to take care of other aspects of her life. Kim neglected the fact that peak performance can only come from a well-rested, happy, healthy athlete. When she relaxed and embraced the dip she was in, her performance improved. There is a reason we have day and night, winter and summer.

George Leonard says:

"Ultimately, practice is the path to mastery. If you stay on it long enough, you will find it to be a vivid place, with ups and downs, its challenges and comforts, surprises, disappointments, and unconditional joys. You'll take your share of bumps and bruises while traveling—bruises of the ego as well as of the body, mind and spirit—but it might well turn out to be the most reliable thing in your life. Then, too, it might eventually make you a winner in your chosen field, if that's what you are looking for, and then people will refer to you as a master. But that's not really the point. What is mastery? At the heart of it, mastery is practice. Mastery is staying on the path."

To make the journey to your mastery more likely to succeed, you need to track your progress. You need to know what is working and what is not working. You need to be able to evaluate objectively all that is happening in your game. This is what we mean when we say that learning is occurring all the time, even when improvement has bogged down. Self-evaluation must never end.

To help you with your evaluation, we have created a special area within our www.vision54.com Web site specifically designed for online learning and self-coaching. This VISION54 online learning center offers tools to track your journey through golf. You'll be able to keep track of what works for you, record your practices, understand your focus, better grasp your tendencies, engage in self-evaluation, and keep track of your statistics.

We have also built into the site learning sessions for the different VISION54 concepts. There is no golf book on the planet that can describe how YOU maximize your potential and play great golf. You need to start creating yours. VISION54.com is here to be your friend on that journey.

The Perfect 30-minute Mastery Practice

- Sit down and think through your game on the course. Answer the questions:

- What do you want to stop doing?

- What do you want to continue doing?

- What do you want to start doing?

- If there is only ONE thing you could do right now to help you on the journey, what would it be?

- Ask someone who knows your game what they see different about you.

CHAPTER XI

Rainy Day Practice

"An investment in knowledge always pays the best
interest."

—BEN FRANKLIN

 SWING KEY: Make the game a part of you—no matter
where you are.

___

There are probably two things on which most golfers
agree: They want to score lower, and they want to
play more. We can help lower your score, but there
is not much we can do about getting you out onto the golf
course with greater frequency. What we can do, however,
is help you learn ways to practice when you are not able
to get to the course. Golf is a game that can always be with
you. And, just as on the practice range, the key to off-
course practice is using your time wisely.

In one of the many commercials Tiger Woods does, the

television camera moves through his house showing the couch, the TV, some photos of his college's sports teams, all while Tiger's voice tells us about the kind of things he would do on a rainy day. Then the camera moves outside and Woods is hitting balls in a driving rain while he says, "Unfortunately, there are no rainy days." While that may be true for those who make a living playing golf, for most who play, the weather or work interferes all too frequently.

But just because you can't get to the golf course doesn't mean you can't practice. There are exercises you can do at home, in a hotel room, or even in your office. The golf course can always be with you, the practice area can always be with you. An important part of the game is in the planning and in the understanding. There are things you can do that will improve your performance on the golf course that don't even involve holding a golf club—or even getting out of a chair.

One of the common traits great players have is an amazing memory. Perhaps it is a function of how intensely they concentrate, but they have staggering recall of shots they have hit. We once heard Byron Nelson describe a shot that his opponent had hit fifty years earlier. Byron knew the club and the yardage—and it wasn't even a shot he hit! While part of that is likely a function of concentration, it is probably also reinforced by thoughtful reconstruction of the round after it is played.

Among the many ways in which Annika Sorenstam exceeds her rivals in preparation is that she is an absolute stat freak. Perhaps that is because her father worked for IBM, but whatever the reason, Annika keeps track of everything she does on the golf course. And she uses that information to get better. She is constantly analyzing the numbers and seeing which part of her game can be improved. When a particular number jumps out at her she focuses on that part of her game. That is something you can do when you are not able to play or practice.

Many people who jog keep a runner's log and record every workout, keeping track of distance, time, weather—everything related to the run. Why don't more golfers do this? Keeping a journal is a great way to become more aware of your tendencies on the golf course. How many fairways did you hit? When you missed, where did you miss? Which were your best shots? How committed did you stay to your shots? How was your focus while swinging? How many putts did you have? How many misses were in a range where you expected to make the putt? Might it be a motivating device inducing you to get better at bunker play if you knew what your success rate was from the sand?

We strongly encourage record keeping in a notebook or on the Track section of the VISION54 Web site. It leads to greater understanding of your game, and **greater understanding leads to better play.** Part of the instruction material students get at our school is a notebook. They are encouraged not just to take notes on the lessons but also to record their performance, their thoughts, and their feelings. What's working? What isn't working? What are you feeling when you execute a shot perfectly? How does that differ from the feeling you have when the execution falls short of your expectation? What is the experience?

In a way, part of what you learn through VISION54 is how to become not only your own golf coach, but also your own best friend. By recording information about your performance, you are encouraging yourself to think more about the game, and that can only lead to better performance.

Let us tell you a tale of two golfers. At the 1994 British Open at Turnberry, Tom Watson played especially well in an early round at a time when he had gone many years without winning. Part of the interview process players go through after a round is to give a shot-by-shot description of their birdies and bogeys. When Watson got to a particular birdie, his face lit up with excitement as he talked about hitting a fade off a hook lie. You could feel how vividly he could see the shot in his mind's eye.

Later that day, John Daly recorded a low score and was also brought into the interview room. As he was going through his birdies and bogeys he stumbled on several occasions, trying to remember the hole. It was a startling contrast between the two men, and likely went a long way toward explaining the fact that Watson was a much more successful player than Daly, even though Daly is a player of considerable skill. Watson's mind was constantly engaged. Daly's was not. That engagement can be learned.

Remember the six elements of golf: Physical, Technical, Mental, Emotional, Social, and Spirit of the game? What would it look like if we charted Tom Watson on a 1-to-5 scale with 5 being the best? Perhaps something like this:

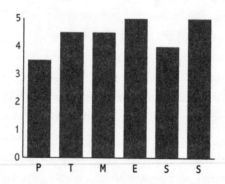

Watson would score very high on his emotional management and his love and passion for the game. That's a large part of why he was such an engaged player and such a great champion. Now, where do we think John Daly would score on such a graph? Perhaps something like this:

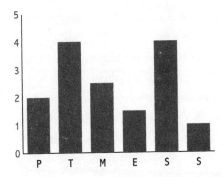

Daly scores high on his technical ability and his social interaction with playing partners and fans, but his emotional swings and lack of intrinsic motivation for the game in part explains his erratic play over the years. Even though he has won two major championships, Daly has only three other victories in his PGA Tour career.

Now, where would you rate yourself in each of the six elements of golf? What do you do well? What could you do better? And how do you go about doing it better?

Besides recording information and experiences, there are other things you can do away from the course that can help your game. Visualization is extremely useful. We have a friend who says he loves to be around good golfers because he feels he gets better though osmosis. In fact, he is probably correct. Watching good players imprints on the brain the image of the proper pass at the golf ball, and when you swing, the brain tries to replicate that action. In a similar vein, thinking about the swing and how you want to swing and play will make you better.

Another friend likes to fall asleep imagining a round on her home course. She imagines where to hit her tee shot and what the approach she faces looks and feels like. She says she carries this imagery onto the course and often ends up playing a hole exactly as she has imagined it. She also says she has conquered some particularly troublesome holes on the course by planning a strategy that made it less fearsome the next time she played it. She was able to hit the shot she imagined hitting.

There are also a lot of physical activities you can do indoors that will improve your game. View time away from the golf course not as a hardship but as an opportunity. That those "off hours" can be used to make you a better player is just one more way in which golf is a unique game, and one more way in which you can experience the joy it brings. As George Leonard says: "Practice mental for physical activities, and practice physical for mental activities."

Here are some examples of how you can do cross training indoors or in your backyard:

- Sit in a chair or lie down and play golf perfectly in your mind and heart. Play one hole or play eighteen holes. Play any course. Be detailed about getting prepared to play, whom you play with, the weather, what you are wearing, what you are feeling, your routines, your presence in the play box, your internal or external talk, the feel of impact, the flight of the ball. Play brilliantly. After the great shots, allow yourself to feel wonderful. Take your time and let your imagination flow. **To be as great as you can be, you want to prepare your whole nervous system for success.** You want your body, mind, and heart to have complete permission to be great. This is a great way to practice it.

- Find a place where you can make swings. Or, if the ceiling is low, cut down an old club so it will be short enough to swing indoors. Make ten swings as slow as you could possibly make them. One swing might take a couple of minutes. On the first three swings, focus on being totally present and aware of your body and swing. Make no judgments; just keep breathing and stay aware. If your mind drifts away, ask it to come back.

  On the next three swings, keep your focus on your tension level. Where is it? In the backswing, is the tension in your lower back? At impact, is the tension in your forearms? How can you make the next swing through those areas with less tension?

  Now make three swings slowly with your eyes closed and stay aware.

  The last swing is of your own choice.

The more intimate you can be with your own body and swing motion, the better player you can become.

You can also try this exercise in front of a mirror. Instead of your internal sensation you will now have an external view.

Here are some more indoor exercises:

- Write down everything you appreciate about yourself, your game, the game of golf, and anything else or anyone else you feel inspired to write about. Take the good feeling into your heart.

- Check your aim with the putter. Do your complete putting routine. Aim toward a coin, the leg of a chair or table. After you aim, put a tee or some kind of triangle across the putter face. Then step back and see if the aiming device is aimed at the target. Do twenty different aims and keep track of the percentage of time you aimed at your intended target.

- Check your pre-swing fundamentals. (Make sure you have communicated with your teacher/coach about what to check on.) In front of a mirror is a great place to check how you put your hands on the club, your posture, the width of your stance, your balance, the distance you stand from the ball, and the ball position in your stance. Do this for full shots, putting, chipping, and pitching.

- Turn a club around and grip it below the clubhead. Swing it five times as fast as you can right-handed then left-handed.

- With your eyes closed and with the golf trail side of your body facing a mirror, swing halfway back. Open your eyes and see if the club is parallel to the ground, parallel to the target line, and the toe of the clubhead is pointing up. Turn around and have the golf lead side of your body facing a mirror. Swing halfway back and then halfway through with your eyes closed and then open them to see if the club is parallel to the ground and parallel to the target line and the clubhead pointing up.

The Perfect 30-minute Indoor Practice

- Make a practice swing with or without a club, standing on one leg, alternating between the left and the right leg. Notice if you can finish in balance. Do this for five minutes.

- Make two slow swings and be aware of the tension level in your body during the swing. Do this for five minutes.

- Check your pre-swing fundamentals in a mirror. How is your grip, stance, posture, etc.?

- Sit down or lie down and imagine you are playing exceptional golf. Do this for ten minutes.

- Look up a rule in the *Rules of Golf* that you are not quite sure of and learn it. Do this for five minutes.

CHAPTER XII

Come Alive in the Play Box

"If I have lost confidence in myself, I have the
universe against me."

—RALPH WALDO EMERSON

 SWING KEY: Great shots result from total engagement.

A friend of ours, Greg, is an actor and avid golfer. He tells a story about being recognized in a restaurant by a fan of his popular television show. The fan, Greg relates, was disappointed that he was not the same person as the character he plays on TV. "That is a person I made up for that role," our friend patiently explained. "Well," said the fan, "he's a lot more interesting than you."

At first Greg was hurt by the comment. Quickly, however, he realized it was a compliment, however unintentional. What the guy was saying was that Greg had created a character so believable it was difficult for the fan to believe that was not who he was. In speaking with our friend about how he created that character each week, we realized there were enormous similarities between being an actor and being a golfer. It's all about total engagement in the play box. And total engagement is something you can practice.

Greg has done a lot of live theater and he told us when he walks onto a stage—even now after nearly thirty years of performing—he still gets goose bumps because he feels he is treading on a special ground where magic is made: the magic of acting. He says that concept is the mental place he goes to get ready for a performance. That mindset—that he is among the fortunate few who get to act as a profession and that he carries on the proud tradition of great actors from the past—helps him achieve peak performance. Greg feels it is his obligation to give the audience his absolute best effort. It is his spiritual connection to his craft.

Anyone who is going to be great at what they do—whether it is being an actor, violinist, surgeon, tennis player, potter, or writer—needs to be able to get into a state of peak performance to maximize their abilities. **Great things are achieved in times of total engagement.** It has been that way for as long as humans have tried to paint, sing, dance, craft fine cabinets, and play golf. To perform at your best, your mind must be locked into the present and your sensory awareness must be fully engaged.

One of the reasons certain players perform so well under pressure is because they love the feelings created by competition. Tiger Woods has said what he enjoys most about being in the heat of competition is that his senses are heightened. And Annika Sorenstam often talks about getting goose bumps when she remembers special shots. "You know what I love," Annika once told us. "I love that feeling when I have a nine-iron in my hand and I have to hit it to two feet." These are two players who allow themselves to get fully engaged in the play box. They don't fear the moment; they embrace it.

When you are ready to perform—ready to hit a golf shot—you enter this state of engagement we refer to as the play box. This is the time frame when you make your total commitment to the activity you are about to perform— hitting a golf shot. You address the ball. You get into your stance. You make your swing. You are on the sacred ground of golf. Performance is state-specific—it is here and now. The play box is state-specific—this shot is all that matters right now. To function well, you want to be in a good state—you want to be right here right now, fully engaged. When it's time to perform you can't change who you are or your skill level. All you can do is commit.

Annika is very clear about her state in the play box. She says: "Behind the ball I see the shot and that vision gives me a feeling for what I need to do. Then I step into the play box with that feeling and swing." When Annika crosses that line into the play box, doubt is left behind. She is totally ready to experience the joy of golf, and completely committed to the process of playing.

Simply put, the play box is the experience of golf. It is alive, compelling, and engaging. It's a first-person experience that is instinctual and rich in sensation. It's the moment of truth. The play box is where your intelligence comes through. It's where you communicate with the target. It's a combination of inner and outer focus. Some people sense that when they play their best they are close to totally outer-focused on the target or ball flight. Others sense that they feel the target and have more inner focus on tempo, grip pressure, or some other swing or body sensation.

How can the target be more compelling than the thoughts in your head? Many of us experience this when we are in the trees and see an opening to go through. Our total focus is on the target, and many players are a lot better in the trees than having an 8-iron left to a wide-open green. This focus can be trained. Some of us get in that state by hitting balls. After a few shots you are fully engaged. What is it for you? And more importantly, how can you create that state of total engagement when you only have one try at the shot?

Greg the actor says he sees a lot of young people who become technically accomplished at their craft but fail to make a spiritual connection with it. In golf, there are many talented players who become so obsessed with the swing, so infatuated with technique, that they direct all their energy toward the mechanical side of the game and none to the performance side. They fail to recognize that golf is both an art and a science. As a result, they become mechanical players capable of making a perfect swing but unlikely to achieve peak-performance golf—especially when it matters most.

How often do you practice achieving such a state of engagement in anything you do? How often do you remind yourself that you play this game because you love it? How often do you let yourself feel the goose bumps? Have you developed an intimate relationship with the game of golf? If not, we highly recommend you check it out. Without knowing how to get in a good state over the ball—a physical, mental, and emotional engagement that will allow peak performance—you will be performing well below your capability.

This is where magic and mystery come into the game of golf. How do you achieve such a peak-performance state? Nobody else can tell you what it is or what it should be for you. It's a first-person experience, not a third-person description. It's an "I" thing or a "me" thing, not a "he or she" thing. It's like the answer trumpet player Louis Armstrong gave when someone asked him what jazz was. "If you have to ask," he said, "you'll never know."

What we can help you learn are the patterns of behavior that will enable you to understand yourself well enough to enter a state of total engagement. When you become aware of what you are looking for, you'll know it when you find it, just like understanding jazz.

A young LPGA player, Helga, came to see us. We have seen her hit many spectacular shots when it really mattered. We asked her to tell us how she does such amazing things. We asked her to explain what her focus is when her awareness is high and she is playing her best. Helga looked up and said, "I don't know. I have never really thought about it."

That was pretty much the answer we expected. So we asked her to ponder the question again, right now, and tell us what her mind locks in on when she is playing great golf.

"Well, I don't know," she repeated. "I don't think about anything." That's a very good answer, and an extremely important piece of information about her relationship to the game.

Helga then said, "I just see it and go and I am not concerned about the score." Wow! What a golden nugget of knowledge in understanding how you function when you are playing great golf, brilliant golf. We can't stress this enough: **One of the most important things to know in golf is how you are when you are great.** How does it feel? How is your focus? What are you aware of? By understanding your state, you make it easier to return to that state.

And that understanding does not have one right answer. It has as many answers as there are individuals with golf clubs in their hands. There is only one of *you* on this planet, and you have a unique and very personal way of experiencing the state of peak performance. You want to discover what it is for you. The key to great golf is being able to repeat your best swings, your best shots. And the first step toward reliable repetition is understanding how you are when you are at your best.

How can you gain that understanding? Pay attention to yourself. After a round, go back to your best shots and note what the experience was like for you. Replay the round in your mind. Write down any "aha!" thoughts you have. You don't want it to stay tacit as knowledge but rather become active understanding.

Some say, "I just grip it and rip it." Others might say, "I feel my hands being all soft and I see my target." Still others might say, "I see the shot happening before I hit it." In all cases, the players are surrendering to the moment, allowing themselves to become totally engaged and totally present in the play box. They are committed to the shot they are about to hit. At that moment in time the shot to be played is the most important thing in the world to them. It is the only thing in the world to them.

What would it mean to be not present in the play box? One example is to be engaged in a conversation with your inner voice. Have you ever stood over a putt and right before stroking the ball said to yourself, "This is for par"? Or perhaps as you settle into your stance on a tee shot the voice says, "I don't want to hit it left again." This is not being present. You are not committed to the shot you are about to hit.

You need to take full control of your golf environment. Keep pollution out of the play box by maintaining total engagement. This will allow you to get in the zone, and when you achieve that state you go from having a sensory experience to having an extrasensory experience. Find out what routine works for you. Annika spends only about four seconds in the play box. Others might spend six or seven, but when you get past eight seconds you've increased the chances for pollution to seep in as doubt.

The act of hitting a golf shot is an incredibly sensual physical activity, not an abstract intellectual exercise. If you are over a shot and the voice says, "I will swing three-quarters and keep my hands ahead of the club at impact," you have moved from a state of sensory awareness into a cognitive state. Your mind is consumed by a "to-do list" instead of engaged with the shot. It's the difference between dancing and talking about dancing. You want to "dance"—swing. Play in the play box to reach your fullest potential.

When you gain a clearer understanding of what the sensory experience is like for you in the play box, the next question is: What do I need to do in the think box to increase the chances I can get into the peak-performance state when I enter the play box? Many golfers learn a "perfect" think box routine and then assume it will lead to a good state in the play box. Understand the difference in how you feel in the play box when you hit a good shot and when you don't hit a good shot. In that understanding you will find your focus.

The Perfect 30-minute Play Box Exercise

Since there is no one right answer to the question of how best to achieve total engagement in the play box, the only sensible exercises involve experimentation with what works best for you. Try these exercises with full swings, putts, chip shots, pitch shots, or any other shot.

- Hum a song in the play box. Does this relax you so you can be fully engaged?

- Count to five while swinging. Does this silence the voice of doubt that creeps into your brain?

- See the ball flight like a red laser beam while you swing. Does this visualization translate into a successful shot for you?

- Use only three or four seconds in the play box without hurrying the shot. Does this help you prevent think box activity from carrying over into the play box?

- Listen to the sound of the swing. Does this make you feel better connected to the shot you are about to hit?

- Sense the grip pressure during the swing. Does this make you aware of how sensual it is to hit a golf shot?

- Feel the center of gravity as being just below your belly button. Does this make you feel grounded and ready to make your best swing?

- See and feel the target being like a magnet. Are you talking to the target? Is it answering back?

CHAPTER XIII

Putt with a Plan

"The art of art, the glory of expression and the sun-
shine of the light of letters, is simplicity."
—WALT WHITMAN

 SWING KEY: Let complexity surrender to simplicity.

---

s Ben Crenshaw walked to the sixteenth green at
Augusta National Golf Club in the final round of
the 1995 Masters, he was carried along by an ova-
tion that brought a tear to the eye of even the most cynical
observer. Just four days after Ben was pallbearer for his
longtime teacher, Harvey Penick, he was authoring a mi-
raculous performance and on his way to winning a tournament in which no one had given him a chance. It was
one of the most memorably emotional moments in the
history of sports.

When the final putt fell, Crenshaw bent over at the

waist, buried his face in his hands, and let the tears flow. Carl Jackson, who had caddied for Ben many times before at the Masters, including in his 1984 victory, put a gentle arm around his old friend and held on until Crenshaw composed himself. There was magic at play that week at Augusta National, and the wand that orchestrated it was Crenshaw's putter. Not once during the seventy-two holes did Gentle Ben three-putt on the treacherous Augusta National greens. Time and again, he maintained momentum with a testy par-saving putt. Crenshaw had always been blessed with uncommon feel in his hands. But Crenshaw feels with his heart as well.

There is no part of the game that we overthink as much as putting, and there is no part of the game with which we struggle as much. Putting is ultimately about getting the ball in the hole. It is the finish line for every hole we play. And perhaps because it is the finish line, we tend to make it more complicated than it is. **The putt is the only shot we hit under the added pressure of being expected to make the shot.** This creates distracting interference.

Watch young people on the greens. Kids putt, adults worry. Kids just look at the hole, respond to what they see and feel, and then stroke the ball. There is little or no interference with the interaction between the child and the hole. There is no outside "noise" keeping them from the task at hand. The intellect is not engaged with how to do it, but rather the intelligence of the child is captivated by the task of getting the ball in the hole.

Adults are too busy doing math to feel the stroke. They are worried about the value of that finish line—the score that will be recorded on the card. All great putters say they putt like a child. Brad Faxon, one of the best putters ever on the PGA Tour, says that if the putt means more to him he's even more "kidlike," actually taking less time over it than normal. Nowhere is the process of golf tested more than in putting. It's the ultimate paradox of outcome versus process. **Commit to the process if you desire the outcome.**

There are a few simple exercises you can do that will serve as excellent maintenance practice for your putting. To make your stroke more fluid, make the stroke in slow motion with your eyes open. Now make it in slow motion with your eyes closed. What do you notice?

A lot of missed putts occur because poor contact is made with the ball. Here's an exercise that will help you make solid contact more often: Put two rubber bands on the putter face only far enough apart for the ball to be struck there. Putt different putts and get a feel for how to find the sweet spot.

You can work on improving your tempo by putting the same putt with different-length strokes. Close your eyes and try to feel the tempo. You can also just putt around the green with the sense of letting go and having no concern about the outcome. Can you feel yourself bonding with the putter and ball?

Part of what made Crenshaw a great putter is that he let very little theory come between himself, his hands, and the club. There is a notion that great putters are born and not made. But even if that is true, poor putters can get better by allowing themselves to get more intuitive, and great putters can get worse if they become too technical. **The key to becoming a better putter is to make putting simple again—as it was when you were a child.**

The game is full of examples of people who do amazing things with the putter when they allow themselves to get lost in the emotion of the moment. At the 2004 U.S. Women's Open, Meg Mallon faced a downhill, fifty-foot birdie putt on the fourth hole of the final round. It seemed more likely she'd putt the ball off the green than two-putt. Instead, Mallon made it, and you could see in her eyes as she walked to the next tee, she knew—she believed—she was going to make every putt that day. And she pretty much did, the clincher being an eighteen-foot par-saver on Number 15 that enabled her to hold off a birdie-birdie finish by Annika Sorenstam and win.

At the 1999 Ryder Cup at The Country Club, great putting became contagious on a team level. Trailing Europe 10–6 going into the final day of singles matches, the United States appeared to have no chance of winning. But

Crenshaw was the captain of the team and he told reporters Saturday evening he believed something magical was going to happen on Sunday. It did. It was almost as if Crenshaw willed his team to putt like him.

Putts started falling and as the roars swept across the course everyone on the U.S. team was caught up in the emotion. The Americans unbelievably won the first seven matches and wrapped up the incredible comeback when Justin Leonard made a forty-footer on Number 17 in his match against José Maria Olazábal. On that day, all twelve Americans believed—felt—they were great putters. And they were. They simplified the process and instead of thinking about putting, they were thinking about making. They were so far behind they had nothing to lose, and they played with that freedom. They became kids again and rediscovered the joy of the game.

Researchers will tell you the act of moving the putter back and through the ball is a less complex motor skill than tying your shoes. Putting puts to its sternest test your view on whether golf is more science or art. You can choose whether you want to "chunk down" and make putting a bunch of numbers, angles, and information; or you can choose to "chunk up" and experience putting as a free-and-easy interaction among the green, the hole, and you.

So what makes up putting? How can we best describe

this childlike process without losing its essence of simplicity? If there is one overriding state you need to achieve when you putt it's this: **Be present! If you aren't aware of the green and how it looks and how it feels, even a technically perfect stroke won't help.** It goes back to a question we asked earlier: **AM I HERE?**

There is perhaps no area of practice where the temptation to get "mindless" is so great as in putting. Ironically, we get mindless by overthinking. We fall in love with putting drills that hide our hearts from our hands. In fact, studies show that practicing the same putt over and over on a chalk line will make you worse, perhaps even creating the dreaded yips. Mindless, repetitive putting will do you more harm than good. Practice being present and free. Practice honoring who you are.

Putting has two components: direction and distance. Long putts are mainly about pace; short putts are mainly about commitment. Decide on direction first. Be completely committed to the line you have chosen. Aim the putter face, and once the putter face is aimed, leave it alone. Never change your decision about the line once you get over the ball. Now all that is left is to commit to the sense of the distance and target.

Distance response is something that lives in the body. It is not an intellectual experience. Get out of your head and into your body when you putt. Do this exercise right now:

PUT THIS BOOK DOWN AND TOSS A WAD OF PAPER AT A TARGET.

You don't even pause to think, do you? Your body knows what to do. The only way you could disrupt this innate intelligence and elegance of motion is to impose an internal dialogue and turn it into an intellectual process by questioning your instincts. How hard should I toss it? Overhand or underhand? Will it curve?

Now let's talk a little mechanics.

Research shows that the face angle of your putter at impact in relation to the target determines where the ball travels. Dave Pelz says a square face angle (perpendicular at impact to the line you have chosen) is five times more important to starting putts on line than the putter path. The shape of the stroke doesn't matter as long as the putter strikes the ball squarely.

When you look at a solidly struck putt you'll discover that the face angle determines 83 percent of the starting line. Pick a line, decide on a speed, commit to those decisions, and then strike the ball squarely. It's as simple as that. Once "aim in the brain" has been completed, then go. BE PRESENT and feel free. Strike the ball squarely.

Pia tells players in the VISION54 programs that she wishes she had trusted this process more when she played the LPGA Tour. Pia had left-brain tendencies when she was on tour and she would read the putt from every angle.

Left-brain players are very rational, linear, well organized. They put their faith in the intellect. Right-brain players go more with their gut feeling. Today Pia putts by being present when she walks up to the green and allows her body and senses to "read" the putt and feel what is supposed to be done. She decides on the direction of the putt from behind the ball and trusts her "aim in the brain." Then she steps into the putt and lets that innate intelligence do its thing.

We tell players that reading greens is overrated. Being present is underrated. If you are present, the green will tell you what to do.

When we ask players how they would putt if there were no "conventional wisdom" on putting, we see some interesting things. They assume a stance and posture that feels natural and comfortable. It always delights us to see, when the "shackles" are taken off their thinking, how free and easy putting becomes. We tend to see putting strokes that resemble the full swing and move in a curve inside to inside rather than straight back and straight through.

We tend to see putter heads that accelerate rather than decelerate. Acceleration happens when we feel comfortable and natural. We don't see people tense in their shoulders trying to keep a perfect V or Y. We see less tension in the hands and more flow and connection with the hole. We see a fluid stroke that likens itself to a child rolling a ball with her hand along the green to the hole. The lesson here is HONOR WHO YOU ARE.

You are going to make the most putts when you honor how you feel and go with it.

The expression "the map is not the territory" is true, but maps often do help you get started in a better direction. A map or guideline for your putting style based on how you sense the world might look like this:

Visual Putters

Visual learners need to see how the putt looks. They like to READ the putt. A visual learner might actually be able to see the green and the break of the putt as three-dimensional. Visual putters lock onto the target quickly and efficiently. That's why visual putters should not read the putt until it is their turn to putt. You want the brain to have a clean, clear image and then putt to what you see in your mind. Visual putters tend to be more upright with their posture and tend to like upright putters. They are more likely to have a straight-back, straight-through stroke. They will say they are aiming for the corner of the hole. The ball is round and the hole is round. There are no corners, but in the visual putter's brain they see it that way!

Auditory Putters

Auditory putters sense the rolling of a round ball to a round hole. They feel the rhythm of the stroke and experience the stroke more like a swinging motion going tick-tock. They sometimes say that every putt has some break to it, that no putt is straight. They might talk to themselves as they size up the putt and sense the break. They might feel the stroke more with their feet and are sensitive to the weight of the putter as it swings. They might sense more of a general target and feel the putt as having balance. They might tend toward more face-balanced putters.

Kinesthetic Putters

Kinesthetic putters feel the putt. They are sensitive to the material of the grip. They need to feel grounded and connected to the hole. They tend to process the putt more slowly than the other two styles and often can't put words to the feeling they have. In a scramble format they don't talk with others about the break. It doesn't make sense to them. It's just a feeling they have, maybe in their hands or stomach or somewhere else.

Kinesthetic putters tend to be "pop" putters and can feel the ball pop off the clubface. If they don't honor their style and sense of feel, they can develop the yips by trying to get too visual and intellectual. For this reason we don't like the saying "reading" putts because it implies that all people see the line, but feeling the line is just as valid a sense of the putt, even if words can't describe it.

Which one do you connect with, or is it a combination?

Left-Eye and Right-Eye Putters

Everyone has a dominant eye and that is an important piece of information to know in putting. Here is a way to determine your eye dominance. Extend both hands forward and place the hands together making a small triangle (approximately ½ to ¾ inch per side) between your thumbs and the first knuckle. With both eyes open, look through the triangle and center something such as a doorknob in the triangle. Close your left eye. If the object remains in view, you are right-eye dominant. If your hands appear to move off the object and move to the left, then you are left-eye dominant.

If you are left-eye dominant, you are already peripherally open to the target and the line of the putt if you play right-handed. If you are right-eye dominant, you might need to adjust your ball position so your right eye is over the ball at address. Generally, this means that a right-eye dominant player will favor a more open stance with the ball farther back. Understanding eye dominance is all part of making certain the real you does the putting.

It is important to remember that the three kinds of practice—warm-up, maintenance, and performance—apply to putting as well. When you warm up, get a feel for pace and stroke. Putt two-footers to create confidence. As for maintenance, aim always needs to be checked. And make certain you are releasing your stroke toward the target. Putt with no think box. For performance practice, putt nine holes and keep score, or make ten different three-footers in a row.

We are amazed how often we see players of all abilities fight against their real self when it comes to putting. We once watched a tour player practice by looking at the hole instead of the ball. The player was putting fifteen-footers and making everything. She made eighty-four consecutive fifteen-foot putts by looking at the hole instead of the ball. The next day, in competition, the player went back to looking at the ball. "Conventional wisdom" is a strong gravitational pull to escape.

Lynn once helped a successful businessman at a VISION-54 program with his putting. He had the dreaded yips. By experimenting he found his most natural stance was putting with his right hand only, with his left hand in his pocket. Just as Lynn and he were finishing the session his wife wandered over and asked how it was going. He demonstrated his new putting style and she shrieked in horror, "You're not going to play in the Pebble Beach Pro-Am like that next week? All of our friends will be watching on TV and I will be so embarrassed." So he went back to his old style—including the yips.

Trusting your senses and feel on the greens is complicated when your instinct opposes conventional wisdom. Malcolm Gladwell, in his book *Blink*, celebrates the power of thinking without thinking. He says great decision-makers aren't those with the most information but those who best filter the very few factors that matter from the large number that don't. This "adaptive unconscious" does a great job of screening the world for us. We think it also can help you putt your very best.

A rookie once asked Nancy Lopez if her caddie read her putts. "No," said Nancy, "he doesn't putt them." Only you can know what you are feeling.

The Perfect 30-minute Putting Practice

- Hit fifty three-footers from different sides of the hole. How many can you make?

- Have someone time you in the play box. How long does it take from when you get settled over the ball until impact? Is it consistent? How long is it when you putt your best?

- Putt a three-footer in four different directions around the hole—north, east, south, and west.

- Putt six different twenty-footers with the goal to get the ball to the hole or a maximum one-putter length past.

- Ask a friend to distract you by talking or putting her shadow in your line. Practice being engaged.

CHAPTER XIV

Get Fit to Play Well

"A sound mind in a sound body is a short but full
description of a happy state in this world."
—JOHN LOCKE,
SEVENTEENTH-CENTURY BRITISH PHILOSOPHER

 SWING KEY: Make your body ready for golf.

There was a time when golfers were not considered
to be athletes. Most participants in other sports, and
many fans as well, felt golfers chose the game because they were simply not gifted enough to play anything
else. That notion has changed in recent years. Participants
at the highest level of golf have learned being fit is part of
being a champion. Fitness is in golf to stay.

Just as Ben Hogan brought the notion that practice was
essential to golf, it was Gary Player in the 1960s who first
introduced the idea that physical conditioning can make

you a better golfer. But for years there was resistance to this idea by those who felt becoming "muscle-bound" would hurt the golf swing. What they failed to understand is that the exercise program must be tailored to the specific needs of golf.

By the time Tiger Woods and Annika Sorenstam hit the scene in the mid-1990s, trainers had developed workout programs directed toward golf. Both Woods and Sorenstam got serious about working out in the late 1990s and their bodies went through remarkable changes. Woods gained more than forty pounds of muscle. Sorenstam's strenuous program added strength and stability to her core and more than thirty yards to her average drive. Other players took notice.

The success of Woods and Sorenstam has attracted a better-quality athlete to golf. Talented youngsters who a generation earlier may have chosen soccer or basketball or tennis now pick golf. Players like Camilo Villegas, whose arms ripple with ropelike muscle, and Lorena Ochoa, who participates in triathlons, changed the look of the game. The professional golfer has evolved into a seriously conditioned athlete.

We tell our students they have two choices when it comes to conditioning. They can make a commitment to become the best golf athlete they can be, or they can accept their level of conditioning and plan their game around what their body will allow. Just be honest with yourself about what level of commitment your schedule and desire will permit.

We see a lot of players who are trying to swing in a way their body can't accommodate. If your body doesn't fit into the cookie cutter, you either have to change your body or change the cookie cutter. Since we don't believe in teaching the same swing to everyone, we totally believe you can find the swing that fits your body. This much is indisputable: Unless your physical stability, strength, and flexibility are integrated with your technical practice and development, the swing will not repeat under the pressure of actual play.

Swing changes are sometimes conceptual adjustments, but most often they are physical deficiencies. Most swing changes that are going to hold up on the golf course are going to require a physical change—either more stability, flexibility, or strength. Have you spent good money taking the same swing lesson over and over again, year after year, with no lasting benefit? It's not as if you don't understand what you're supposed to do. The truth is your body can't do it consistently or under pressure on the golf course.

Maria, a long-time VISION54 student, noticed that under pressure she had a tendency to pull her irons. She understood she was coming over the top from a technical perspective. But the baffling part was why it would suddenly show up. We checked Maria's ability to keep her upper body still and rotate her lower body. She had very limited range of motion. When tired or under pressure, the weakest link (physically, mentally, or emotionally) in the system will show up. Instead of working on the technique, Maria focused on her hip mobility in order to perform better under pressure.

The swing must fit the body and the body must fit the swing. Great ball strikers have very different swings, but they also have a very similar kinematic sequence, which can be analyzed on video. The sequence of the lower body, torso, arms, and hands at impact stays the same. Great ball strikers have a wide variety of swings, which we can easily see by looking at two-dimensional videos of Tiger Woods, Ernie Els, Lorena Ochoa, Annika Sorenstam, or Colin Montgomerie. But they also have very similar kinematic sequences, which can also be analyzed on a three-dimensional video. The sequence of the trunk, upper body, arms, and the hands at impact is the same.

What should you do if you are interested in changing your body? Our advice is to have a trainer evaluate your conditioning and give you specific exercises. The Titleist Performance Institute is a great resource. They have gathered many of the best minds in golf fitness, and have devised proven ways to evaluate players and develop exercises tailored to the individual.

A couple of simple screenings can get you started doing a self-evaluation: Can you touch your toes without bending your legs? Can you dissociate your lower and upper body? With your arms across the chest, get in a 6-iron position. Keeping the lower body still, can you rotate the upper body? Now do the opposite. Keep your upper body still and rotate your hips. With the club up over your head can you go down in a full squat without bending forward with your arms? If you have problems with any of these, it will affect your swing technique. You will be required to make compensations in your swing to hit the ball properly.

The key to training is "scalability." Determine what works for you and for the level of commitment you are willing to make. Kai Fusser, the instructor who has directed Sorenstam's workout program, says he teaches a thirteen-year-old and a sixty-three-year-old the same workout he teaches Annika. "It's just a matter of the intensity," Fusser says.

Some players have time to work out several times a week, and others might be able to exercise only once a week. But the key is to do something. That's why scalability is crucial. What should you do if you have only one minute to work out? How about if you have ten minutes, or thirty minutes, or an hour? The important thing is to get in the habit of cross training for golf. Like practice itself, the amount of time you commit is not as important as making the commitment and being consistent.

First, you want to create functional movements in your body, and then it's a lot easier to have a functional golf swing. We also feel it's important to combine exercises that are slow with a great inner awareness and with exercises that are fast and more robust. The inner and outer balance of your body is a wonderful asset to great golf.

Dr. Greg Rose at Titleist Performance Institute says that the glutes (the butt) are the king of golf and the abs (the stomach) are the queen. These muscles can develop a strong, stable core around which a solid, repeating swing can rotate. **To maximize your ROI from your work-outs, concentrate on the core.** But this can vary from person to person. Get a good screening and find out your weakest link physically and work on it.

By learning more about the connection between the body and the swing, we have had great realizations about our own swings. Lynn has always had a tendency to sway in the backswing. Then recently Lynn realized she was physically incapable of stabilizing her lower body and thus fully rotating her upper body in the backswing because of a lack of glute strength! Practice won't help until she gets physically stronger in that area.

Pia has always had a tendency to lose her posture at impact. Her butt gets closer to the ball at impact than when the swing is started. Practice hasn't been enough. On the course, when it matters, the tendency is still there. Finally, Pia realized she was too tight in the hip flexors and lower back and too weak in the abs. This has made it impossible to hold the posture at impact.

Remember, as with all aspects of your game, fitness has

the warm-up, maintenance, and performance components as well. Just as you learn what works best to warm up for a round of golf, you'll learn what works best to get you ready for a workout. Maintenance can be as simple as staying well hydrated and engaging in aerobic exercises that develop stability, flexibility, and strength. All of this is certainly part of your preparation practice. Be patient. Improvement takes time.

Fusser has identified three principles he feels must be involved with every exercise toward building a body designed for golf:

• Feel the ground

• Stay aligned

• Abs in

These three elements have to work together just like the body parts need to work together to execute a successful athletic move. "Every time you neglect one principle in any way you take away some percentage of a 100 percent perfect move," Fusser says. In the golf swing, power is produced through the activation of *all* the muscles in the body; not one muscle will be left out during the performance of the swing. Here's how to build a solid foundation for a solid swing:

Standing with a solid base and straight spine, pull your

belly button in and up. You will feel some pressure against your lower spine from the stomach wall pushing back. You might also feel your rib cage has lifted some and the breathing might be a little restricted. That's normal until you learn how to dissociate your core from the upper body. Try to relax the upper and lower body adjacent to your midsection so they can move freely while your core is tight. This will take some time and practice, but once achieved it will make a huge difference in your stability and strength.

There are two good ways to practice this:

Stand with your heels, glutes, shoulders, and head resting against the wall. Place one hand behind the small of your back and draw your belly button in and up against the wall. Feel the pressure against your hand.

In this position, learn to relax the rest of your body and try to breathe relaxed as well. Hold for twenty to thirty seconds, let go and rest for ten to twenty seconds. Repeat this four or five times.

The second way is to get into the above position and again pull the abs in with the rest of the body relaxed. Now rotate your upper body from one side to the other, with your arms freely hanging. If you are relaxed your arms should swing freely in front of you through the rotational forces while your core remains tight throughout.

This "abs in" engagement needs to be started before

any movement. Fusser refers to the belly button as the "start button" that has to be pushed in before beginning any move, no matter how simple.

Nutrition and hydration are exceedingly complex areas of attention that are probably the most personal. Our main point for nutrition on the golf course is to keep an even energy level during the round. Soft drinks and candy bars don't help, since they trigger sugar "rushes" and the eventual sugar "crash" that create uneven energy levels.

As for hydration, the nutritionist Robert Yang suggests a water intake equal in ounces to one half the body weight. If you weigh 180 pounds you should consume ninety ounces of water a day. Of course, if you are playing in the Arizona desert in August you'll need to increase your intake.

The Perfect 30-minute Workout Practice

- Lie on your back and put your hands on your belly below the belly button. Focus on your breathing. Feel your hands rise as you inhale and go down as you exhale. Sense your own being and the breaths flowing through your body. Now add a feeling of appreciation from the heart. Remember, getting in touch with yourself, allowing your body, mind, and heart to get on the same page, is a huge part of getting stronger, because a fully integrated being functions the most efficiently. Do this for five minutes.

- From this same position move your hands, arms, legs, and feet as slowly as you can in any direction. The key here is to stay present and awake. Remain in the now, fully focused on what you are doing. The nature of the exact movement is not as important as being connected to the movement. Pretend you are doing slow-motion snow angels. Feel your body move. You will be surprised how much this will help you in feeling your body and allowing it to make a golf swing that works for you. Do this for five minutes.

- Now that you have said hello to your body and introduced it to your heart and mind, stand up and make a slow-motion golf swing without a club and with your eyes closed. Keep your mind focused on what you are doing. Think of the golf swing as a dance movement to the slowest, most graceful melody. Feel your swing. This is YOUR swing. No one else has one like it. Get to know it. Celebrate it! Do this for five minutes.

- Now that you have slowed down the pace of the world, now that you have integrated the head, heart, and body, let's increase the tempo a little bit. Jumping rope is a very good aerobic exercise. If you don't have a jump rope, pretend you do, or replace it with jumping jacks. Do this for three minutes.

- Get on all fours with your thighs and arms perpendicular to the floor as we create the "cat and dog" position. Without bending your elbows, try to lower your spine, creating the dog position, and then lift or arch your spine up to create the cat position. Repeat a few times and then find the neutral position.

- Now that your heart is thumping, bring your mind back to golf. Stand at the address position for what would be a 6-iron shot. Cross your arms over your chest with your hands resting on your shoulders, as if you are giving yourself a hug. Keeping your lower body still, rotate the upper body into a backswing position and then into a follow-through position. Can you feel your body functioning as an integrated unit? Do this for two minutes.

- Remember, the butt and the abs are the king and queen of the swing. Let's work on those muscles. Stand up and do deep knee-bend squats. Keep your mind focused on your balance and allow yourself to feel the muscles work. Find a rhythm and pace that is comfortable for you. Do this for three minutes.

These exercises can be done by anyone, but always make certain to do only what your body allows you to do. These exercises also do not involve complicated or expensive workout equipment. Just as we think it is important to demystify golf instruction, we think it is also important to demystify physical instruction. It's all about getting the heart, mind, and body on the same page.

For those of you who feel that one way you can get your biggest ROI is through better conditioning, we recommend finding a good golf fitness instructor who can build a program that fits you.

CHAPTER XV

Bake the Cake of Confidence

"When you have confidence, you can have a lot of
fun. And when you have fun, you can do amazing things."

—JOE NAMATH

 SWING KEY: Don't wait for it to happen. Make it
happen.

When Annika Sorenstam won the U.S. Women's
Open in 1996 for the second consecutive year,
most who follow the game closely would have
predicted she'd win the American national championship
a half dozen more times. Annika appeared to have the perfect U.S. Open game: astonishing control with both her
shots and her emotions. But, for a variety of reasons—
among them a final round 66 by Juli Inkster one year and

a closing 65 by Meg Mallon in another—it would be ten years before Sorenstam lifted that large winner's trophy for a third time. When Annika finally won the Open again, she was using her VISION54 skills.

The first thing Annika said after that triumph at the 2006 U.S. Women's Open at Newport Country Club following an eighteen-hole playoff with Pat Hurst was: "I must have looked funny out there this week, since I talked to myself constantly. I just needed to remind myself all week to stay focused on each shot. I wanted to win so badly that my mind wanted to run ahead. I kept saying to myself how much this means and to stay committed to every shot. Today, every shot truly had a purpose."

Of course Annika has the skill level needed to win, and no one came into the tournament better prepared. Still, even if you are Annika Sorenstam you need to nurture the other factors that influence confidence and give the possibility of great performance. Because Annika had her heart broken in the U.S. Open before, and because she views it as the most difficult (and therefore the most important) tournament to win, she entered with added pressure on her sturdy shoulders. Even a player as accomplished as Annika can have doubts. Fortunately, she has learned how to handle those doubts with a hardwired memory of past successes.

Even professionals tend to look at confidence as a gift

rather than a reward for consistent, conscious habits. While not everyone can be an Annika Sorenstam, everyone can learn how to put in the effort needed to reap the reward of confidence. It's a feeling everyone who has played the game has experienced at one time or another—the sensation when you absolutely know in your heart of hearts the shot you are about to hit is going to be perfect. The great players know how to make that feeling a frequent visitor.

One of the things we do when we conduct a VISION-54 golf class is to ask each of the individuals what they want to accomplish through our program. Almost all say they want to get more confident. But if we think that way it will be an extremely difficult goal to achieve. Confidence is not a commodity you can go to the store and pick up, but rather it is a state of being you need to create. **We can't get confidence, but we can learn how to create it.** Those people who appear to be supremely confident are not the lucky recipients of a fortunate gift but rather the clever folks who have figured out what works for them that allows them to create a state of confidence.

At times you are fortunate and some external factor will make you experience confidence. Maybe a playing partner compliments your swing or gushes about how far you hit a drive. Maybe your swing teacher says your backswing position is perfect. Or perhaps you one-putt the first three holes. When things like this happen, it is a huge boost to your confidence. But what if you are not fortunate enough to have confidence handed to you on a silver platter?

The answer is to learn how to create confidence from within. Since you always have yourself with you, wouldn't it be great if you could become your own best confidence coach? Wouldn't it be great if you could access confidence whenever you needed it? It is an achievable goal. All you need is the right tools, and a purposeful approach.

You see great players like Tiger and Annika creating confidence for themselves all the time when they are in stressful situations. It's one of the reasons they have won so many tournaments, and a reason they are so successful in the major championships. When they are under pressure they have positive experiences in the past with which to associate, and they know how to access those memories. That's why often a player who has struggled to get her first victory suddenly has a wave of victories. She now has a memory of how to win.

Being confident is not a static state. It's very dynamic. Confidence does not descend from without but rather emerges from within. Think of it not as the inhale, but as the exhale. But as important as it is to create confidence, most players give it no attention. They think of that state of being as something unattainable, something that only the special players have.

Truthfully, how often do you train and nurture this ability to create confidence that is vital for great golf performance? For most players the answer is not at all. So how do you create confidence? Let's imagine that you are going to bake a cake called "confidence." What kind of ingredients would it have?

Some of the more important ones are:

- Emotional stored memory (Remember past successes.)

- Skill level (Realistically assess your competence in all aspects of golf.)

- Self-talk (Is your inner monologue positive or negative? What and how do you talk to yourself?)

- Body posture (Walk like a champion.)

- Preparation (Have you had proper rest, nutrition, warm-up, and sufficient quantity and quality of practice?)

- Focus on things under your control (Don't get distracted by those things you can't control. If it's windy, it's windy for everybody. You can't control the weather.)

- Your beliefs about yourself, the game, your swing, your performance (What beliefs do you have that are helpful and you want to keep? Do you have any beliefs you want to change?)

- Ability to create a state of peak performance (How engaged are you in the play box?)

Start with this as your confidence checklist. Now grade yourself on each of these areas, giving a 1 if you feel your competence in the area is low and a 5 if you feel it is high. How can you train yourself to improve the ones you mark low? What do you need to do to nurture what you are already good at and make it even better? Again, it's all about being specific. What do you need to do, and what plan do you need to develop to achieve your goal? Now have someone who knows your game grade you.

A major component in the effort to create confidence is controlling self-talk. All of us have self-talk. This is the inner monologue we carry on all the time. Studies say we have at least sixty thousand thoughts a day. And more than 90 percent of those thoughts are the same as the day before. The question is, what quality does your self-talk have? Is it your best friend? Are you being your own best coach? Or are you speaking destructively to yourself?

We all have thoughts, but we believe we are not our thoughts. That's all they are—merely thoughts, not reality. Those thoughts are not who you are. You control that. The number-one rule is: You don't have to believe what that inner voice is saying to you. If it says, "I never play this hole well," reason with it. Prove it wrong. Tell it the past doesn't have to be the future. Become expert at replacing destructive inner monologues with more useful conversations.

Kevin, a young playing pro we have been coaching, was concerned he would have funny thoughts on the course in competition. It could be things like "I will miss this putt" or "I am three under par already; I wonder if I will hold up." Kevin thought there was something wrong with him for having these thoughts. We told him we don't know any player who doesn't have funny thoughts pop up in their mind. Knowing that the thoughts are not him, that they are just thoughts, made him take a deep, comforting breath. Now when Kevin competes and the thoughts appear, he just says this mantra to himself: "Kevin, it's just a thought, not you. Where is the target?"

We had another student, Nick, who realized he had two different voices inside of him. One was nurturing and one was very critical. Now he is aware which one is good to have on the golf course. He has learned to listen to the friendly voice and tone down or replace the destructive one. We all have succeeded and we all have failed on the golf course. Which memory should we train our inner monologue to remind us about?

We often film students when they play and we are able to show them how, on different holes, they change their body language from one of confidence to one that is tentative and unsure. The players are shocked the confident body posture looks so good. In their internal experience doing it, they thought it would look strange and cocky! Remember, don't use the video camera only for analyzing the golf swing. You can also use it to analyze your attitude on the golf course.

Another very interesting exercise is to pay attention to what you say to yourself on the golf course, and how you express those thoughts. This is an exercise you can do with a friend. Make a deal that whatever you say to yourself between the shots, you will say out loud. You can also do this exercise alone. Bring a notebook with you and write down what the inner voice is saying. Some of the players we work with talk into a tape recorder and listen to it after the round to evaluate the quality of their inner monologue.

The supremely confident play a lot like those actors or musicians who emerge as "overnight successes." When we look more closely we find that they have been creating and accumulating many good habits for many years to get the success that has suddenly emerged. And so it is with the confident player. They didn't find confidence, they created it.

The Perfect 30-minute Confidence Exercise

- Spend thirty minutes focusing entirely on your body language and your self-talk while you practice on the range or putting green. If you were the best player in the world, how would you walk, stand, step into the ball? What would you say to yourself and how would you say it?

Or

- Make twenty two-footers. Hear, see, and feel the ball go into the hole.

- Hit your favorite club on the range for ten minutes, using your complete think box/play box routine for each shot.

- Spend five minutes imagining yourself playing great golf. See, feel, and hear yourself walking, swinging, putting, etc., with the posture, self-talk, technique, and focus you want to have when you are as good as you can be.

- Write down the five most important things you can do to nurture your self-confidence.

CHAPTER XVI

Know Yourself to Play Better

"Knowing others is intelligence, knowing yourself
is true wisdom; mastering others is strength, mastering yourself is true power."

—*Tao Te Ching*

SWING KEY: You are the master of your life.

One of the observations we have about the way golf instruction has evolved is that the pendulum has swung more toward the "science" side of the game and away from the "art" side. This obsession with the golf swing minimizes the human element. And part of what makes golf so enjoyable and so challenging is that it is a very human game that, when experienced to its fullest, puts us in greater touch with ourselves. The game is played not in a laboratory but in the world.

When the game has been reduced to swing planes and

spine angles it loses some of its joy, and it ill prepares us for taking the game from the practice range into the real world. We see it time and again: Those players bogged down with checklists and to-do lists can be thrown out of their comfort zone when confronted with the fact they have to face people, places, and situations they cannot control. The have not been taught how to handle those situations. They don't know how to respond when the voice of distraction calls.

- "I can't play with him because he talks too much."

- "I can't play with her because her routines are so slow."

- "I can't stand when the course maintenance crew is in my way when I play."

- "I can't hit it well off the first hole, since there are other people watching."

- "My spouse gives me advice on every single hole and it drives my crazy."

- "My caddie should be in a better mood and know when to make a joke."

We hear complaints like this all the time. But golf is a part of life—your life—and living involves interaction with others. Even for those with legendary concentration—Hogan, Sorenstam, Woods, Nicklaus—the game is never played in a vacuum. To perform your best, you need to learn how to be yourself while at the same time interacting with others. You need to respect yourself, but you also need to respect those you play with. We all tend to project our irritations onto those around us, but what good is that?

Take control! You are the expert on you and nobody else. You are the CEO of your life and your golf game. If you have people that distract you in golf, ask yourself these questions:

What do you appreciate about these people?

What would you like to be different?

How could you communicate this to them?

Are there too many people involved? Is there someone you want to eliminate? Is there someone you don't trust in your golf relationships? Most of the time when players lose trust in others it is because of poor communication. We tend to make the erroneous assumption that others know what we are thinking, and then we get frustrated because they cannot read our minds. Dealing with annoying situations doesn't mean you have to be rude. You can do it with a smile. It might take practice, but it can be done. You decide. It is your game.

Through the years we have done many training sessions for club, college, or national teams. The amount of talking behind the backs of teammates and the degree to which it disturbs both enjoyment and performance is surprising and significant. Take care of the team of which you are a part and it will nurture good performance. **When you engage in undermining others, you are also undermining your own performance.**

One growing concern we have had in recent years is the large number of junior golfers who never learn to take responsibility for their own games. This often happens because well-intentioned parents insist on continuing their role as the CEO of their child's golf game. And to play your best golf, you need to own your own experience and be empowered from within. To play your best, you need to be intimate with your own thoughts, tempo, and feelings. This can't happen if the parents remain as a suffocating presence.

It seems obvious to us: If someone else is telling you what to think, feel, and do, you will not develop the skill to be your own best coach. Golf is played with me, myself, and I as a team in the act of hitting golf shots to targets. Some years back, the American Junior Golf Association asked us to write a booklet for parents about how to support their young player, and what tools are necessary to make it more likely that support will happen. Clearly, the AJGA recognized a problem.

A tricky situation is coping with an annoying person you don't know very well. How do you get them to stop? The first step is to accept that there is nothing you can do about their behavior. But you can learn to manage your own state. You can't change them, but you can change how you react to them. If players talking during your routine bothers you, if slow play bothers you, if negative playing partners bother you, invite these distractions into your practice and learn to deal with them, learn how to return to your own performance state even with distractions swirling around you.

If slow play, for example, bothers you, first find out how you react when play is slow.

- Do you change your routines?

- Does your mind go crazy with judgments about the other players in the group?

- Does your body get tense?

If you are aware your routines have been thrown off, deal with that. Don't waste energy being annoyed at the other person's behavior; direct that energy instead to returning to your proper state. You determine your routines, no one else. Don't allow yourself to suddenly take two minutes to prepare for a shot when your normal routine is thirty seconds. Don't rush your routine to make up for others. If your routine takes twenty-five seconds, for example, you will never be considered a slow player.

If your mind is going crazy with negative thoughts, distract it by humming a song or any other activity that can refocus your thoughts. If your body is getting tense or your tempo too quick, relax your body or focus on making swings with a slower tempo.

This is the only strategy we know that works for things that are out of our control. Quit complaining, face it, and figure out what you can do to coach yourself. The blame game never works. A key component to good golf is energy management. Don't give it away.

Two other self-coaching tools:

Learn the difference between being associated and dissociated.

You are associated when you are experiencing a situation and feeling it. "Why are you slicing the ball?" your spouse is asking, and the anger starts boiling inside of you. You are dissociated when you experience a situation from the outside with no feelings. You are like an objective scientist. You see your spouse as if he/she were on a TV screen asking you the same question. It's a very different internal experience. Some days you might need this skill a lot to better deal with situations that otherwise would irritate you and influence your performance ability. Learn to associate with the positive experiences and dissociate from the negative ones.

Learn to separate what you see and hear from your opinions, judgments, assumptions, and interpretations about what is happening.

A playing partner might tell you that you look nervous, and it's annoying since you are not nervous. So you get upset at what was said. With this skill you would know better. You can ask instead, "What makes you think I am nervous? What have you heard or seen?" Your playing partner might say, "You seem so quiet and you are walking faster than normal." Then you can answer, "Thanks for telling me, but it has nothing to do with being nervous."

A few times we have heard Annika say, when asked who she is paired with: "I don't know and it doesn't matter because I am going to play my own game." Other players will make a big deal out of it if they have a good pairing or if they are with someone with whom they do not enjoy playing.

As a young player, Annika used to get very annoyed if she had to swing or putt through her own shadow. If she had a late tee time, she would know in advance which holes might be bad. In talking about it, she agreed it is a good thing to have late tee times on the weekend. It's nothing you want to avoid. Face it instead. She started practicing on purpose with the shadow in the way, to figure out how to get back to her own performance state.

We have learned a very usable practice from Ken Wilber's *Integral Life Practice* called the 3-2-1 process. According to Wilber, an important aspect of an integrated practice is to have a way to be profoundly honest with ourselves about people, places, and situations that annoy us. These annoyances sometimes become a blind spot. But we push the annoyance outside of ourselves, often onto someone else. You can only let go of that which you first own. The 3-2-1 process uses a shift in perspective as a way of identifying and integrating things that bother you. The 3-2-1 refers to third-person, second-person, and first-person perspective. This is how it works:

Take any situation or person that annoys, irritates, or worries you. There are three steps: **FACE IT, TALK TO IT, AND BE IT.**

Sit down, close your eyes, and take a few deep breaths. First, imagine yourself in a third-person experience of the situation. Face it. You see, hear, and feel this annoying situation or person. Spend some time doing that.

Next, you want to get a second-person experience of the situation. Talk to it. Imagine yourself conversing with the person or people about the situation. What do you say? What do you ask? What will the others ask you? Spend some time doing that.

Lastly, you go into a first-person experience of the situation. Be it. Speak as the other person or people. Imagine yourself being the annoyance. Describe the "I" feeling and wants. Integrate that with your own "I." Spend some time doing that. What comes out of it?

What would be a GOLF 3-2-1 example? Perhaps you get irritated over slow play and you know you are paired with two players who are slow-play criminals. Doing this GOLF 3-2-1, you would first imagine what it's like playing with them. Face it. Imagine the whole situation.

Next you imagine yourself communicating with the two players. Talk to it. Perhaps you say, "You two are the slowest players at the club, and do you realize how hard it is for me and many others to play with you? Have you ever thought about being ready when it's your turn and making your routines a little quicker?" One of the players might respond, "Nobody has ever said that before. I just want to make sure I am totally prepared before hitting a shot. Personally, I think that you are too stressed out there."

The third step would be to imagine you having the problem yourself. Be it. Take the other person's perspective. "I am slow, and it's just because I want to do my very best."

By engaging in this exercise, you can learn to understand your own behavior better and also gain a better understanding of the feelings and behavior of others. And greater understanding always leads to greater control. You will learn not to waste time and energy worrying about others but rather direct that energy into managing your own behavior. Ultimately, that is all you can control.

The Perfect 30-minute Social Practice

• Do the GOLF 3-2-1 exercise.

• Replay your last round of golf and replay ten shots being associated and ten shots being dissociated.

• Pick one thing that annoys you and create the situation in a practice situation to learn how you can deal with it differently.

CHAPTER XVII

Nurture Your Passion for the Game

"The best and most beautiful things in the world cannot be seen or even touched; they must be felt by the heart."

—HELEN KELLER

 SWING KEY: Know the reason you play the game.

One of the things that makes life such a fun adventure is that no two of us ever experience any event in exactly the same way. All that goes on in this wonderful world passes through one undeniable filter—us. It is our senses, our brain, and our heart that determine the beauty of a sunset. No two people see it the same way. Some squeeze every ounce of joy possible out of the experience, while others view it merely as the end of the day. The same is true with golf. We all experience the game differently.

The spirit of the game—the passion we bring to the process—is often overlooked as a key component in performance. Rarely are you asked why you play this game. Or, more importantly, "What about this game brings you joy?" If you can't identify your areas of joy, you have lost your connection to the game. You have lost sight of the fact that it is something you "play," and not something you merely work at.

We believe identifying a person's area of passion—the source of their spirit in the game—is essential in maximizing their performance as a player. We see students of all levels—junior golfers, professionals, club amateurs, and seniors—who have no air left in the tire. The spirit that gives shape to their game has seeped out little by little until they become lifeless shadows of their self, sleepwalking through golf. When love of the game is lost, the bar of achievement is greatly lowered.

To find your passion, you need to recognize it when it arrives. Pay attention to what it feels like when you have that special spark inside. Make notes when it happens. Over time you will start to see a trend of what components need to be in place for you to experience the true spirit of the game. Ask people close to you to point it out when you are having fun with the game. What needs to be different for you to experience it more often?

After Lynn's parents retired they started playing more golf together. After the first hole, Lynn's dad would ask her mom, "Bunky, what did you have?" The reply would be something like: "Oooh, Ducky, I don't know, give me a seven." That would elicit the response: "Give me a seven! What does that mean, don't you keep score? If you don't keep score I can't beat you!" Ducky's spirit of the game was the thrill of competition, while Bunky's was for social reasons and to enjoy the beauty of nature.

There are a wide variety of reasons people play the game. Some people play just to get a college scholarship, while for others it is because they are urged by a spouse or a parent. For some professionals it's merely about being famous or making lots of money. While these extrinsic reasons can inspire a player in the short run, they are usually not sustainable long-term motivations for playing the game.

Focusing only on extrinsic goals will not lead you to the best possible golf. It's OK to play to win, or to play to make your family happy, or to get a juicy paycheck, but only as long as your own spirit of the game is also nurtured and fully alive. To stay in touch with this spirit and to help it flourish, it is essential to understand what it is about the game that makes you want to play it.

- What about this royal and ancient game gives you energy?

- What about your golf experiences makes you want to come back and play again?

- What fuels your golf engine?

- What is compelling, joyful, enchanting about the game for you?

This spirit is the life force that binds all the other parts of golf together; it is the glue that connects you to the process of playing. For some, this spirit comes from the joy of sharing fun with friends. For others, it emanates from communing with nature and knowing that every golf course on the planet looks and feels different, and that even the same course will have a different character from day to day.

Still others find joy in knowing the journey through golf never ends. There is no destination but rather the constant challenge of improving. There are those, also, who love the adrenaline rush that comes with the thrill of competition, or those who get their pleasure from the social interaction. The list is endless, but the key is to know what it means for you. Like the game itself, this evaluation is an endless process. **Life changes and so do the reasons you play the game.**

Dr. Joan Duda at the University of Birmingham is an expert on the role of motivation in sports and, with her colleagues, has conducted years of study on Olympic athletes. She told us they used to think it was the athlete who wanted to win the most who had the greatest motivation. Now they know that it's actually the balance of the extrinsic (winning) motivation and the intrinsic motivation that best allows success to unfold. The intrinsic motivation is what we call spirit of the game. This spirit is what you like about the experience of golf—the playing of the game—independent of the outcome. The more you understand what needs golf fulfills in you, the better you will perform.

We have supported many professionals who had lost touch with their spirit of the game. All of them knew in their hearts that no matter how well they swing, or how perfect their ball flight is, or how physically strong they become, there is still something missing, an emptiness, a void. There was something intangible that couldn't be filled with another swing theory or another "tweak of the week." The spark was missing from their experience.

One of these lost players realized that her passion for the game had died because she did not have a life outside of golf. Being with her boyfriend and shopping is what she really liked. Another tour player lost her spirit because she was exhausted from never taking time off and from always being judged by her family because of her scores.

A young male pro said as a junior he used to have fun

with golf, creating all kinds of practice games with his friends and mixing the golf games with hacky sack and skateboarding. As a professional he had stopped those fun games. He thought he needed to be "serious" and just hit balls on the range and iron his pants so he would fit in.

Another world-class player realized that her life is totally different now from ten years ago. She has more varied interests than when she first came on tour. She still wants to compete at the highest level, but she wants to do so within the context of her life now. To do that she has to re-evaluate her relationship with golf and redefine her passion for the game. The center of her spirit in the game has shifted.

The essential question you have to ask is how golf makes sense in your life. What needs to be different for golf to be meaningful and fit into your life?

Among the players we have coached are several good amateurs who really looked forward to retirement because they would have more time for golf. But after a few months of retirement, they had transferred their work energy and obsession to golf. And when they started "work golf" the fun part of the game faded away and their handicap went up.

We highly suggest that your spirit of the game—that

about golf which brings you satisfaction—includes more than low scores and winning. You can influence scoring and winning, but you can't control it, and that is a fact that can easily dampen your spirit. Another way to say it is to learn to separate what you do from who you are. Separate your love for the game from the scoring of the game.

Players will always have ups and downs when it comes to performance. That is the nature of the game and also the natural cycle of life. Players who cannot maintain their self-esteem at a base level during the "down" times will have trouble sustaining motivation and energy. They need to find and nurture the pure enjoyment of playing the game with all of its inherent challenges, dips, and plateaus. The same goes for the superstars on tour. They also need to be seen for who they ARE, not always for what they DO.

With more teenagers turning professional so early, we have seen the spirit of the game overlooked by many eager and excited parents. Getting good at a young age is seen as a race. We had a twenty-five-year-old player we coach tell us she felt like one of the old women on tour. Parents, beware! If the spirit of the game is not nurtured it won't matter how much money sponsors are willing to pay and how much money you think your son or daughter can make in professional golf. And it won't matter how much talent they have. Success will not be sustainable.

This is a game that can last a lifetime, and the joy of the

game—your joy of the game—needs to be individually located and uniquely explored.

The score will always be there on the card, but the opportunity for learning and insight will be greatly increased by shifting your evaluation of the experience from the quantitative outcome to a reflection on process. The answers for the future of your game might reveal themselves as you look deeper and wider than just the number you posted. At the very least, it's a more interesting conversation, and it will produce a healthier perspective about you and your experience in golf.

You are a human being who plays golf, not a golfer who happens to be a human being. Your past is important, but it is not nearly as important to your present as the way you see your future. What you achieve is affected by what you believe you can achieve. The more you are in touch with your spirit in the game—the passion and love you have for golf—the higher your beliefs will soar, and the better you will perform.

Next time you play, keep an energy scorecard. If you start with $100 worth of energy on the first tee, mark down after each hole how much you have left. The goal would be to have $100 or more when you walk off the final green. If that's not the case, ask yourself what you need to do differently to change your emotional bottom line. When you finish a round of golf, you should feel you can't wait to play again, not as if you have been run through a wringer. It's all about finding your pure center, your love of the game of golf.

The Perfect 30-minute Spirit of the Game Practice

Start a journal where you keep checking in with yourself and answering questions like:

- What interests you about golf?

- What makes you want to jump out of bed in the morning and play or practice?

- When you first started playing golf, what was fun about it?

- What makes you unique as a golfer?

- What do you like about the game?

- What gives you the most energy in golf?

- How do you want to be as a golfer?

- If anything could be different, what would make golf more fun for you?

- What is it in golf that makes you grow as a golfer and human being?

- Ask someone who plays with you often to tell you when they see you most enjoying yourself on the golf course.

CHAPTER XVIII

Celebrate Golf: Sing the Song of Greatness

"Yes, to dance beneath the diamond sky with one
hand waving free, silhouetted by the sea . . ."

—Bob Dylan

 SWING KEY: Let your conversation with the game begin.

G olf gets lost at times in a one-way conversation in which the language of one of our most ancient sports is muted by efforts to explain the unexplainable—the magic that occurs when human, club, ball, nature, and the course merge into the glorious act of a well-struck shot. A better balance needs to be reached between the art and science of the game.

Watch young children dance. They do so with no fear of judgment, and with no knowledge of the rules. They just feel the music and move. That is the way we experience the game of golf when we learn it at a young age. The child grabs the clubs, looks at the target and the ball on the ground, and swings. If he or she hits it, there is a squeal of delight. Often, even a swing and a miss brings laughter. The process is not cluttered by thought, doubts, expectations, or judgments. It is a game and everything about it is fun.

Those stories of Tiger Woods sitting in a high chair in the family garage as an infant and watching his father swing a club never say anything about Earl Woods burdening the visual lessons with verbal baggage. Sure, some instruction came later, but at the beginning, Tiger just watched and moved to the rhythm of the game. He remains now one of the most instinctual players ever to play the game. There is a lot of golf in Tiger's head, but there is even more of the game in his heart.

As we grow older we lose trust in our instincts and become more aware of the way things are "supposed" to be done. What was a child's game becomes an adult's chore. We lose sight of the fact that the challenges that make golf difficult are the essence of the sport that allow it to offer up its greatest rewards and make it a game for life. Golf is a wonderfully complex game best experienced when viewed as a friend to caress and not an obstacle to conquer. Don't fight it. Love it.

Listen! Let the game speak to you. What does it say

about itself? What does it tell you about yourself? If you have a conversation with the game, you just might hear it tell you how you need to play, and how you need to practice. Most of the exercises we have shared with you in this book have as their purpose to make you a technically better player by making you less technical. Most of the exercises here are about breaking down the wall between you and the game, between instruction and play, between art and science.

The evolution of golf into more a science than an art has been a gradual phenomenon that has accelerated in recent years. The early architects of instruction understood the oneness of the game. They got it.

In his book *Swing the Clubhead* published in 1952, Ernest Jones wrote: **"It is the mind which interferes with the business of swinging a golf club by introducing so many extraneous factors which do nothing but interfere with the swing."**

The 1922 book *Golf Fundamentals* by Seymour Dunn states: "Leave theory in your locker and play naturally."

And *The Art of Golf*, published in 1887 by Sir W. G. Simpson, Captain of the Honourable Company of Edinburgh Golfers, reduces golf to its bare essence: "Now golf is a game in which each player has a small hard ball of his own, which he strikes with a stick whilst it is quiescent, with the intention of putting it into a hole. Abstractly he wishes to do this with as few blows as possible, concretely in fewer than his opponent."

Why make it any more complicated than that? Just get the ball in the hole in as few strokes as possible, preferably fewer than the other people against whom you are competing. That message has been drowned out by the drone of instruction. But the beauty of the joy still whispers in the wind.

You need to listen to the game, and you need to listen to yourself. Since it's you who will play the game of golf, you need to be aware of the state you are in when you play, and from that you will learn how to manage your state so you can get more enjoyment out of playing the game. You, the clubs, the ball, and the course need to play well together as a team.

Golf today is mostly looked at from the chunked-down details of the grip, stance, and length of backswing. This school of thought says that if you get all the details of the swing down you will play good golf. Our experience is that that approach doesn't work very well.

How would it be if we did the opposite? Let's look at the beauty of the whole game, not just the swing. Let's look at the beauty of YOU playing this ancient game, not you struggling to form perfect angles with your arms. No one can become great at any activity if they do not love the activity. Let yourself love the game—experience the inside of the game, feel the beat of its heart—and you will find the lessons you need to get better.

Practice for us is intentional growth. If you want to get better at golf, your practice needs to take the broadest possible look at the game. It must embrace the whole game—the physical, technical, mental, emotional, social, and spirit of the game. If you are honest with yourself you will admit that your greatest shots came in moments when you were so connected with the game, you were virtually unaware of making the swing or stroke. What you practice you get good at. Be careful what you choose to do in practice.

Whenever we see truly great performances—Jack Nicklaus in the 1986 Masters, Tiger Woods at the 2000 U.S. Open, Annika Sorenstam when she shot 59—there is a sense something more is going on than just the physical. There is a sense something magical is happening. And it is. The athletes have merged as one with the game they are playing. Peak performance is the perfect wedding of the physical, technical, mental, emotional, social, and your spirit of the game.

The first doorway to joy in the game of golf is marked "understanding." Understand the game. Understand yourself in the game. And, perhaps most importantly, understand what you want out of the game. Understand how you play great golf. Get intimate knowledge of how you function when you are great. If you don't know that, you don't know what to go toward. After looking at the full scope of the game, find your ROI.

Those who want to be the best need to commit to quality practice in sufficient quantity and for a number of years. That's how you get to be the best. Those who are not going to make that effort have to find their joy by having realistic expectations of what they can get out of the game, based on what they are willing to put into it.

But no matter what level of commitment you are willing to make to practice, don't get stuck limiting your notion of practice to a series of unconnected activities: driving, iron play, fairway woods, wedges, short game, putting, and so on. You need competence in all the different skills of golf, and that competence is achieved not by compartmentalizing instruction but rather by breaking down the walls and experiencing the whole game.

If there is one message we hope you take away from this book, it is that you can achieve peak performance. It is in all of us. You can become competent in how to create a state of peak performance. You can learn how you function when you are great, and you can learn how you get in your own way when you are not. From this understanding you can identify how you can get better.

We each have our own answer for the question concerning the meaning of *The Game Before the Game*. Lynn feels that by reading the book you will feel *compelled* by the experience of practice. The game before the game tugs at your heart. The joy of discovering your game is pulling you, not pushing you. You are motivated to develop *all* that you are.

Pia says the short-term intention of the book is to learn how to get in the state of peak performance with the skill level you have. How can you get in the best state possible for your skill level? Long term, it's all about having the broad view of the game, finding your ROI and taking action to maximize it. As golf coaches, we both see this book as a celebration of the VISION54 mission, which is to bring possibility to life.

What are you going to do with all you have read? Hopefully, you have learned that your best golf is waiting to be discovered. Hopefully, what you have read has demonstrated the need to span the width of the golf experience in your preparation and practice. To those who ask if golf is a physical or a mental activity, we reply this way: neither. Golf is so much richer than that. It is physical, it is mental, but it is also magical. There is an element to the game that is beyond explanation, and that is part of what we love about golf.

All the factors involved in the game influence one another all the time. If you don't span the width of golf but focus only on being mentally great, you will not be able to play the best possible golf. If you only focus on having the greatest technique ever, you will not be able to play up to your potential. Establish a broad width of perspective and then go as deep in each area as you can, using your goals as well as your time and energy available as the blueprint for how far you dig.

In many ways, understanding all we have written in this book is the booby prize. It is only part of the answer. Action is what will shift your paradigm and improve the future of your game.

With fun and well-thought-out practice, you can make a lot of things happen in thirty-minute practice sessions done regularly. You can even get a lot out of a shorter session if it is done properly. If there is a final message we want you to get from this book it is that peak performance is more likely to happen when you allow yourself to have fun playing the game. You'll play your best when you learn to "dance beneath the diamond sky with one hand waving free." You'll play your best when you remember what it felt like to dance when you knew no rules except this one: Enjoy!

The Perfect 30-minute Celebration Practice

- Write down three beliefs about you or the game that serve or support your intentions in golf.

- Write down three beliefs that you have about yourself or the game of golf that you want to change, delete, or review.

- Hit one good wedge.

- Hit one good 7-iron.

- Hit one good driver.

- Hit one good 9-iron.

- Hit one good shot with a club of your choice.

- Hit one good three-footer.

- Hit one good thirty-footer.

- Hit one good chip shot.

- Hit one good pitch shot.

- Hit one good bunker shot.

- Enjoy each one of them!

Explore The World of VISION54 Principles

Now that you've been introduced to *The Game Before the Game*, VISION54 invites you to further explore how to bring your own possibility to life with an integrated approach to learning the game of golf. By visiting VISION54.com, you'll discover a wealth of tools you can use to become your own best coach and to continue with a lifetime of improvement and enjoyment in golf.

Within VISION54.com, be sure to check out the VISION54 Online Learning Center, an area of our site that features digital downloads, learning sessions, interactive coaching exercises, and online self-evaluation tools.

You'll also find details and schedules of the variety of VISION54 Golf Programs, presenting you with the opportunity for multiday integrated coaching experiences with VISION54 cofounders Lynn Marriott and Pia Nilsson.